e2
effectiveelders

FOREWORD

"If I could have read this book years ago, the churches I have served would have been much more effective for our Lord and I would have left a stronger legacy of leadership." I wrote that statement immediately after reading the manuscript. It was my first thought.

These writers seem to realize that there are many who have somewhat the same feelings and they offer us sound teaching concerning the training of elders and other church leaders. Their writing provides us with a valuable course of study for this endeavor. They present some fine, basic resource material for the church that desires to break away from old traditions and return to the older traditional leadership of nearly two thousand years ago. We must remember that a return to New Testament leadership will propel our congregations into New Testament evangelism, discipleship, and service.

Our authors have mastered the use of the word of God in their teaching. Nearly every main point is backed up with quote after quote from the Bible. No one can accuse them of serving up their own ideas and opinions. Here is Scriptural teaching at its best. They help us apply their concepts with the use of excellent illustrations, many of which are taken from the Bible and some are from our own culture. Regardless of the source, the illustrations and stories that are presented capture our interest and broaden our understanding.

This book offers an honest appraisal of the average American church and points out that much of our failure is the result of poor leadership. Our authors go on to destroy our excuses, push our own ideas, myths, and believable lies off to the side. They offer us a bright hope for the future of the church and prove that things will become better as we build quality into church leadership groups.

The "Reflection Questions" that are found in every chapter will become a catalyst for self-examination. The reader is led to honestly evaluate the purpose of his congregation as well as the ability of his own elders and leaders. If the questions are considered with honesty and concern, they can become a launching pad for the process of planning and implementing needed change and outreach.

The responsibilities of elders and leaders are defined in very understandable ways. The elder is pictured as a lifetime learner, one who becomes a wall to stop false teachers and false doctrine. Therefore, the elder must be not only a spiritual man, but also a man of ability who truly wants to serve in the local church. He must be one who leads out in ministry and service. In my own work with small churches, I have concluded that many leaders do not want to lead. They want to control. This attitude among elders and leaders will keep others from serving. The result is smallness in attitudes, ministries, evangelism, and attendance. I thank God for the teaching material of this book. It will help leaders to break out of the prison of a mentality that limits what God will do through their congregation for the community in which they exist.

Over the years, my own experiences in working with elders and other leaders has been more than satisfying. I often give thanks to God for the fine men with whom I have served. The heartbreaking, spirit-rending stories I have heard other ministers discuss have never been a part of my life as a preacher. However, I have often suffered from those surges of guilt that come from the realization that I have done very little to develop and promote an effective training program for the leaders who have meant so much to my ministry. "If I could have read this book years ago . . ." I've already said that, haven't I?

Jim Estep, David Roadcup, and Gary Johnson have given us a "how-to" book that contains a well-outlined curriculum for leadership development. So, let us thank God for these three men who have taken the time and made the effort to make this book available today.

Ben Merold
St. Charles, MO

Lead

Table of Contents

Introduction

Introduction to *Lead*

I like church potlucks! Tables spread with everything people can bring to the table. You can smell the aroma before you even get to the fellowship hall. However, as an experienced "potlucker" I also know that what everyone brings to the table is not of equal quality. We tend to rush to those dishes prepared by the cooks best recognized by the church, and perhaps take a small portion for kindness sake from the person not quite gifted with culinary skills. (There's nothing worse than having an entire, untouched casserole to take home after a church potluck.)

Serving as an elder within the congregation, you have to ask, "What do I bring to the leadership table?" What competencies do I have to share in the ministry of God's Kingdom? Without competency, the eldership becomes a ineffective gathering of men who have little to contribute to the church's ministry table. Called? Yes. Character? Yes. But without *competencies*, you are not able to lead effectively or efficiently. This book looks at the competencies essential to serving as an elder.

Healthy congregations require a healthy leadership. Without a healthy leadership, the odds of a congregation growing spiritually, let alone numerically, are greatly diminished. This is the principle concern of this series: Healthy leadership facilitates healthy congregational life. To ensure healthy congregations, we must give attention to the health of our leadership, the elders. This book endeavors to orient, inform, challenge, educate, and ultimately equip men to be leaders within the congregation, elders that genuinely lead and shepherd the flock of God. It calls us to reflect in our character the character of Christ while serving as elders within His body.

Leadership that is Christian is based on God's *call* to service, one to which we must *Answer*. The man is qualified and equipped by a life representative of Christian *character*, maturity, we *Reflect His character*. Further, an elder must possess *competencies*, abilities that serve him well as he leads and shepherds God's people; *Lead* His congregation. Finally, the *community*, both the congregation and its social context, provide the area for an elder to serve as a leader within the community of faith and a witness to the community around it as we *Enjoy* His people. All four are essential for Christian leadership to be effective, none of them are optional.

About the Series

This book is the second of a four volume designed to equip elders for effective leadership in the congregation by e2 ministries (www.e2elders.org). The four volumes (*Answer, Reflect, Lead, and Enjoy*) parallel the four basic components of Christian leadership previously explained. These books are not intended to be scholarly treatises of the eldership. Rather, they are designed as *useful study guides* that utilize practical and academic insights to provide a "manual" to the eldership. Each chapter is intentionally brief and concludes with reflective questions for your own personal use, or use as an eldership as a means of training and equipping one another for service.

Lead, Volume 3, addresses the skills or competencies of an elder as a leader in the congregation and community. Chapter 1 "Looking Within" addresses the internal growth of a leader, especially as a learner, enabling the elder to become an effective teacher. The next two chapters, "Looking Around" and "Looking Ahead" address two critical leadership skills for elders; decision making and strategic planning, respectively. The much needed art of mentoring and discipling is explained in Chapter 4 "Taking Under Wing", while the elder's ministry of shepherding and providing Godly counsel is highlighted in Chapter 5 "Taking Alongside". The final chapter, "Taking to Task", explains the unfortunately necessity of church discipline, an often neglected dimension of an elder's work.

This book can be used in two ways. First, it can be used as an individual study, something that you as an individual elder within the congregation read for your own edification and education. You may be a new elder, or perhaps an experienced leader looking for additional perspective and insight. Regardless, this book integrates throughout the text a set of Reflection Questions designed to help you apply each chapter to your life as a Christian and an elder. A second way in which this book can be used is by your eldership. Each elder could read the book, use the Reflection Questions, but then make use of them to discuss the text together as an eldership. In either case, whether individual or group, we do hope the book is beneficial to your life and ministry.

About the Authors

This series is not the product of one author. Rather, it is the fruit of three individuals' labor, working in concert with one another, and bringing their diverse experience and perspective to the table for discussion. One of the authors is a churchman, Gary Johnson (Indianapolis Colts fan), another is a church

Dave   Gary   Jim
January 15, 2010

consultant, David Roadcup (Cincinnati Bengals fan), and still another is an academic, James Estep (Chicago Bears fan). In spite of the rivalries and upsets of the football season, they were able to come together and write the book. While these three men have known one another separately for a long time, it was not until they were all three together in Heiligenkreuz, Austria teaching students from eastern Europe and central Asia at *Haus Edelweiss* (TCMI) that the three men sat together for the first time and shared their concerns for the health of congregations and the health of its leadership. We are convinced that a healthy leadership builds a healthy congregation. From these initial conversations over coffee a hemisphere away came the idea for this series, designed to strengthen the health of elders as the congregation's leaders. It further led to the founding of e2: effective elders ministries in June 2012 (www.e2elders.org).

While individuals were assigned their own chapters to write, the final form of each chapter was reviewed and reworked by all three authors sharing a common table, typically in Indianapolis, Indiana. Hence, the work is a tri-authored resource for the equipping of congregational leaders who serve as elders of the Church.

We are praying for you and your congregation, and if we may be of service, feel free to contact us at your convenience.

July 2013

James Estep, Jr., Ph.D.
Dean, School of
Undergraduate Studies
Lincoln Christian
University
Lincoln, Illinois
Jim@e2elders.org

David Roadcup, D.Min.
Professor of Christian
Ministries
Cincinnati Christian
University
Cincinnati, Ohio
David@e2elders.org

Gary Johnson, D.Min.
Senior Minister
Indian Creek Christian
Church
Indianapolis, Indiana
Gary@e2elders.org

Chapter 1

Look Within: Leading through Learning

James Riley Estep, Jr.

"Be . . . all that you can be . . . in the Army." With this slogan the United States Army recruited hundreds of thousands of young men and women to serve their country throughout the 1980s and 1990s. It held the promise of fulfilling one's potential, maximizing skills, and becoming something more than what you are at present. There was more to serving as a solider than acquiring a set of skills and a uniform, they wanted you to *be* a soldier . . . the rest would come naturally.

Elders are expected to "be" many things. In fact, as one peruses the list of life qualities they are not asked to do much, but they have to possess many qualities. However, in terms of what an elder has to be able to do is "teach" (1 Tim. 3:2; Titus 1:9). Developing the inner life of the elder has already been addressed in the first two volumes in this series, in terms of calling and character. However, before a elder can be a leader, he must first become a learner. For one to lead through teaching, he must develop a teachable spirit, one that is able to learn.

🏴 **Reflection Question:** What is the most intimidating factor about being a teacher? What is it that makes you question your teaching abilities?

Elders as Teachers

"For Ezra had devoted himself to the study and observance of the Law of the Lord, and to teaching its decrees and laws in Israel" (Ezra 7:10). While Ezra is not a New Testament elder, he is indeed an elder of Israel, one of the leaders who led them home to Judea from generation of exile in Babylon. Notice that before teaching, he "devoted himself to the study and observance of the Law." Teaching begins with an inner journey of devotion, study, and observance. I actually appreciate some of the subtle differences with this passage in the King James Version, "For Ezra had *prepared his heart* to *seek* the law of the Lord, and *to do it*, and to teach in Israel statutes and judgments" (KJV). Teaching is not just standing behind a lectern and sharing our insights and opinions, although that is what it can appear to be. It is the result of a prepared heart that didn't just study once, but seeks out the truth of God's Word and puts it into practice, exemplifying its instruction. Having been processed through the heart, mind, and life of the Christian, he is now ready to teach it to others. Elders, as teachers of the congregation, must cultivate these qualities in their lives if they are to lead effectively.

Reflection Question: How would you describe your passion for learning? How devoted are you to study and observation of God's Word?

"The elders who direct the affairs of the church well are worthy of double honor, especially those whose work is preaching and teaching" (1 Tim. 5:17). The New Testament explains not only that an elder is to teach (1 Tim 3:2, Titus 1:9), but why an elder must teach. The most immediate need is to affirm the faithful and defend against false teaching (Acts 20:28-31). Paul explains to Titus on Crete that an elder, "He must hold firmly to the trustworthy message as it has been taught, so that he can encourage others by sound doctrine and refute those who oppose it" (Titus 1:9). On the contrary, the false teachers they must oppose are described as "For there are many rebellious people, mere talkers and deceivers, especially those of the circumcision group. They must be silenced, because they are ruining whole households by teaching things they ought not to teach — and that for the sake of dishonest gain" (Titus 1:10, 11). Just as in the first century A.D., Christian leaders today must be capable of defending the faith and the faithful against those who seek to malign and squelch the Church's faith.

An elder needs a depth of understanding and experience to lead a congregation effectively. As Paul instructed the Ephesians, " It was he who gave some to be . . . pastors and teachers, to prepare God's people for works of service, so that the body of Christ may be built up . . ." (Eph. 4:11-12). This requires that elders not only develop the life of a learner and the practice of a teacher, but to enable others to do the same. "And the things you have heard me say in the presence of many witnesses entrust to reliable men who will also be qualified to teach others" (2 Tim. 2:2). This is probably why an elder cannot be a new convert, since leadership in the church requires not only advanced knowledge but significant Christian experience to match (1 Tim. 3:6). C. Robert Wetzel, former President of Emmanuel School of Religions, in reflecting on his time in ministry said of the elders with whom he served, "They never stopped teaching me."[1] An elder must first be a learner before he is a leader.

Reflection Question: Read 1 Timothy 3. Compare the lives, messages, and faith of those who are faithful teachers of God's Word with those who are not.

Elder as a Life-Long Learner

I've been an elder for over 20 years, haven't I already learned enough to be an elder? Why is it necessary for elders to be learners? Haven't I already learned enough just to become an elder? The attitude reflected in such statements would beg to say . . . No. Elders must aspire to be lifelong learners; ones who are never simply satisfied with their current level of learning, nor do they perceive the eldership as the "end" of the learning road.

☞ Reflection Question: What objections to "learning" have you heard (or even used)? Why could someone consider "beyond" the need for further instruction?

Elders should exemplify the spirit of Apollos in Acts 18. He is described as being "a Jew . . . a native of Alexandria, came to Ephesus. He was a *learned man*, with a *thorough knowledge of the Scriptures*. He had been *instructed in the way of the Lord*, and he spoke with great fervor and taught *about Jesus accurately*, <u>though he knew only the baptism of John</u>" (Acts 18:24-25). Lesson to be learned: *No one knows everything*. Apollos was obviously open to the instruction of Priscilla and Aquila when "they invited him to their home and explained to him the way of God more adequately" (Acts 18:26). He obviously possessed a teachable spirit, one that placed a premium on learning. In spite of his lofty depiction, he was aware that he was in need of further instruction, and was open to it.

Scripture does indeed portray the elder as a man of the mind; one who has the genuine capacity to think, both practically and theologically. This characteristic is seen in the various life qualifications and leadership skills that describe the ministry of the elder. Elders are perhaps best described in this regard as *practical theologians*. By qualification and practice, the elder must know the truth, be able to defend it against false teaching, guard the church and his own family from error and teach it within the congregation (Titus 1:6, 9; Eph. 4:12-13; 1 Tim. 3:2; Acts 20:17-36).

Scripture would refer to this kind of thinking as *wisdom*. Wisdom is more than knowledge, it is the ability to apply God's perspective to life situations (Lk. 21:15; 1 Cor. 12:8; Eph. 1:17). In the Old Testament, such books as Ecclesiastes, Proverbs, and Job are wisdom literature; as they provide spiritual insight and principles into the issues of daily life. In the New Testament, James is one who best reflects this idea of wisdom.

> If any of you lacks wisdom, he should ask God, who gives generously to all without finding fault, and it will be given to him. But when he asks, he must believe and not doubt, because he who doubts is like a wave of the sea, blown and tossed by the wind. That man should not think he will receive anything from the Lord; he is a double-minded man, unstable in all he does (James 1:5-8).

. . . .

> Who is wise and understanding among you? *Let him show it by his good life, by deeds done in the humility that comes from wisdom.* But if you harbor bitter envy and selfish ambition in your hearts, do not boast about it or deny the truth. Such "wisdom" does not come down from heaven but is earthly, unspiritual, of the devil. For where you have envy and selfish ambition, there you find disorder and every evil practice. But the wisdom that comes from heaven is first of all pure; then peace-loving, considerate, submissive, full of mercy and good fruit, impartial and sincere. Peacemakers who sow in peace raise a harvest of righteousness (James 3:13-18 emphasis added).

Notice the connection between possessing wisdom and reflecting God's character in your life. Elders must become proficient in exercising Godly wisdom, the wisdom from above; while avoiding the ungodly wisdom. Benjamin Bloom, an educational theorist, suggested that cognition, thinking, occurs on six levels, ranging from rote memorization to what he called "evaluation," which can be described as one's ability appraise, assess, choose and compare

15

options, defend decisions, judge, predict, rate, value, and evaluate.[2] This is a portrait of what Scripture calls *wisdom*.

🏳 **Reflection Question:** When would such abilities to think, to exercise wisdom, been helpful as a leader in your congregation? When was a lack of wisdom a detriment to the eldership's ability to lead?

Leading, Learning and Teaching

Few people in the world today don't recognize the name "Apple" and its all too familiar logo of a once-bitten apple (painful as it may be for an avid PC fan to admit). From a garage in southern California, Stephen Jobs built Apple Corporation into what it is today, and rose to be one of the youngest CEOs of a Fortune 500 company that continues to be technologically innovative and a hi-tech trend setter. In 1983 when asked about leadership at Apple, he said, "We went through that stage in Apple where we went out and thought we're going to be a big company let's hire professional management, we went out and hired professional management, it didn't work at all. Most of them were bozos. They knew how to manage, but they didn't know how to do anything. And so if you're a great person why do you want to work for someone you cannot learn anything from?"[3] Unintentionally, Stephen Jobs affirms the principle of the leader-as-learner/teacher that God has for the eldership. Teaching, predicated on a lifelong pursuit of learning, is a viable means of exerting leadership within the congregation.

How can teaching serve as a stance for leadership? Leadership can be enacted through several means, such as positional authority, shear power, personal manipulation, charismatic popularity . . . all of which are not necessarily suited for God's Kingdom. Leadership that is enacted through instruction relies on key elements that are suggested by Ezra. First, *heart-set*. An elders devotion to God's Word must be seen by those around him. He must characterize what it means to be a student of Scripture, a life-long learner. As such, he leads by example. Second, *mind-set*. If an elder is to lead through teaching, the elder must be knowledgeable about the subject. In this case, ignorance is neither bliss nor an ally. Yet, an elder cannot simply possess facts of a subject, but must be able to process it into usable information. An elder leads through the recognition of his knowledge and wisdom. Third, *life-set*. As mentioned in the second volume of this series, character is critical for an elder. However, in this context, character is the result of a life-application process of God's truth. An elder first practices God's instruction before passing it along to another, so that it is not mere content that is being shared, but Christian faith and life itself. An elder leads through living out what he teaches, serving as an exemplar for the Christian faith. *Finally*, as Ezra indicates, he must be able to *skill-set*. The ability to accurately and relevantly communicate God's Truth to a congregation and community is essential for Christian leadership. When an elder possesses all these skills, in increasing measure, they are capable of leading the congregation through the art of instruction.

Reflection Question: Based on the previous section, assess your "sets" on a scale of 1-5 (1 being low and 5 being high) and offer an example or reason for giving the rating.

Item	Rating	Comments?
Heart-set	① ② ③ ④ ⑤	
Mind-set	① ② ③ ④ ⑤	
Life-set	① ② ③ ④ ⑤	
Skill-set	① ② ③ ④ ⑤	

When Elders Don't Learn-Teach

When elders are not learners and thinkers, they are forced to rely on tradition. "We've always done it this way" or the more common, "We've never done it that way before." *Learning precludes the blind dominance of unquestioned tradition*. Perhaps there is no better demonstration of the need for a thinking leadership than in Acts 15, wherein a decision must be rendered regarding Paul's Gentile mission. The matter before them was indeed one of both theological and practical significance. Could Gentiles enter the Church without first converting to Judaism? Is it indeed sufficient to affirm Christ as Savior, or is affirmation of the Mosaic law a prerequisite? This was a question requiring a theologically informed practical response. In this instance, "the apostles *and elders* met to consider this question. After *much discussion*, . . ." (15:6-7a, emphasis added) a decision was indeed rendered. Notice that the apostles alone did not engage in the discussion, but included the elders from the congregations. Likewise, Acts 15 records those who made significant contributions to the discussion, starting with Peter (vv. 7-11), followed by the leaders of the Gentile mission itself, Barnabas and Paul (v. 12). However, the final address is delivered by James (vv. 13-21), one that seems to have provided the definitive perspective on the subject. Why is this important? James is not an apostle, nor was he a member of the first missionary journey to the Gentiles; and hence he was probably a recognized church leader . . . an elder.[4] The narrative closes with, "Then the apostles *and elders*, with the whole church, decided . . ." (Acts 15:22a) to send a letter detailing their decision on the matter.

What is the point? It is c. A.D. 50. Tradition was non-existent, and even if they could, the church had never previously encountered an issue such as this. They could have appealed strictly to the available Scriptures, the Old Testament, and probably have affirmed the position of those *objecting* to Paul and Barnabas' mission. They could have responded, "We've never done it this way before!" but that wouldn't have answered the question (frankly, it never does; it the way you were doing it actually worked, the problem or situation wouldn't have developed in the first place). Even with the presence of the apostles, the practical dimension of the issue required discussion as to the appropriate application of their theological convictions. The point is this: *Church leaders have to think!* The apostles and elders had to understand and analyze the circumstances, make the appropriate application of Scripture and their theological convictions, and finally formulate a plan for addressing the issue. They had to demonstrate the capacity to exercise genuine wisdom as described in Scripture.

Reflection Question: When has tradition triumphed over thinking? When has taboo prohibited informed dialogue on the subject? How has this impacted the leadership of the eldership?

A Learning-Teaching Plan for Elders

If elders are going to be thinkers, they need to have a knowledge base. "Do your best to present yourself to God as one approved, a workman who does not need to be ashamed and who correctly handles the word of truth" (2 Tim. 2:15). They have to be students of five areas of study. These five areas form the core essentials with which elders should be acquainted. No, it's not as if elders are expected to be Bible college or seminary graduates, but as leaders of the congregation they should be at least *familiar* with these five areas so as to serve as informed leaders. *First,* elders need to know and be known to their congregations. This may sound like an assumption, but I am also aware that some elders seclude themselves from the congregation to the extent that they are not readily recognized as congregational leaders, or they are detached from the life of the congregation. Elders should be informed of the congregation's current health, as well as knowledgeable of needs within the congregation. To do so, elders must actively engage the congregation, be open and available to them. Ministers can likewise inform elders, and even encourage elders to participate in acts of ministry to specific members.

Second, elders should have grounding in Scripture and theology. This is specifically expressed in the qualifications for serving as an elder. If elders are to defend the faith and instruct others in it, it presumes that they are knowledgeable of it. This requires elders to demonstrate their proficiency in biblical knowledge and the theology of our movement. How can elders be expected to engage in theological reflection if they do not have sufficient biblical or theological knowledge. Bible surveys as well as introductions to theology are readily available from any number of publishers (including College Press's *Simple* series) that can provide a sound start to an elder's spiritual intellect.

Next, elders should embrace our Restoration Movement heritage. We are not a denomination in the typical sense of the word, but we are likewise not simply generic or "non-denominational" in the sense that we have no heritage. Rather, we have a history as well as principles that have guided our movement since its inception. For example, "In essentials, unity; in opinion, liberty; but in all things, love." Not only knowing the principle, but also how it has been applied throughout the decades helps an elder know what it means to be part of our Restoration heritage; which in turn helps us make the application of biblical and theological truth. Most college and seminaries affiliated with our churches offer courses on campus, on-line, or via correspondence in which elders could audit. Likewise, books that concisely present the history of our movement are available, such as James North's *Union in Truth* (College Press) or his history of the church in *Pentecost to Present* (College Press).

Fourth, elders should understand their current culture. Not the culture in which they were born, nor the one they grew up in, or any time of the past; but the current culture. When I went into youth ministry, it was 1985. I remember reading a popular news magazine's treatment of teen culture, with pictures of adolescents dressed like  Cindy Lauper and members of a punk rock band. If I reentered the youth ministry today or approach my incoming freshman class as if nothing had changed since 1985 . . . my ministry would be an anachronism, belonging more in a museum than a church. It would be like trying to navigate the roadways of Chicago using a map from 1951. *Even if the map were accurate, it is simply outdated.* Elders must understand the current culture to understand how to reach out to it and minister in it more effectively. Committing to watch news, televised documentaries, or even reading news magazines that not only give news, but analyze it as well are very helpful in this regard.

Finally, elders should become students of ministry. Many times, an elder's experience of ministry is limited to the congregation in which they serve, or perhaps within a congregation similar to the one they now serve. Hence, new ideas or changes are often difficult to comprehend because of our own experiential barriers. This may not even require doing additional reading or watching videos, but rather visiting other congregations. When on vacation, visit a congregation larger than your own, and don't hesitate to ask questions of the ministry staff after the service. Pick up literature from other congregations, subscribe to their newsletters, or even surf the internet looking for congregations that may provide insight for your congregation's next step. Many colleges, seminaries, larger congregations, and the North American Christian Convention offer workshops or conferences for church leaders, and especially elders.

Developing a Learning Team

No one elder could expect to be an "expert" on any one of these five areas. Of course, God in His wisdom did not appoint one-elder leadership, but rather a plurality of elders who can share their insights and thoughts. Thinking as a team, brining to the table their own expertise and experience. How can this be developed?

Many elders choose to read a book jointly with one another, spending time during the elders meeting (or even over a meal) discussing the assigned reading. The same could be done by providing one another with CDs of lectures, books on tape, conference workshops for elders to listen too would also facilitate the same. Retreats for elders, either sponsored by the congregation or even conferences sponsored by others, provide excellent opportunities for elderships to collaborate in a learning environment. Many of our institutions of higher education and publishers sponsor conferences for church leaders, as well as workshops presented at the North American Christian Convention and National Missionary Convention may be very beneficial to elders.

The critical matter is developing a DNA among the eldership that is intentional about learning. An eldership committed to learning is one that is always thinking, growing, and offering fresh biblical perspectives on the contemporary matters confronting the church.

Reflection Question: Use a piece of paper to write a paragraph plan for studying in the five areas just discussed. How will you begin to move along the learning curve? How might you as an eldership jointly develop a learning culture among the eldership?

Endnotes

[1] C. Robert Wetzel, "They Never Stopped Teaching Me," *Christian Standard*, May 2, 2008, pp. 5-7.

[2] Cf. Benjamin S. Bloom, *Taxonomy of Educational Objectives: Book 1 – Cognitive Domain.* (White Plains, New York: Longman, 1956).

[3] Stephen Jobs interview on video: "In Search of Excellence," (John Nathan and Sam Tyler Productions, 1986). Available through Enterprise Media.

[4] Cf. Eckhard J. Schnabel, *Early Christian Mission, Volume 1: Jesus and the Twelve* (Downer's Grove, Illinois: InterVarsity Press, 2004), 431-435.

Chapter 2

Looking Around: Leading Through Analytical Thinking & Decision Making

Gary L. Johnson

"Shoot for the moon.
Even if you miss you'll be among the stars."
Les Brown

There is a great truth: "we are fearfully and wonderfully made" (Ps. 139:14). David, the psalmist, could not have said it better. Our creation is beyond explanation, and our human bodies are a world unto themselves. Dr. Gerhard Dirks developed computer memory systems, and he indicated that if a computer were designed to imitate the function of the human brain, that one computer would be housed in a twenty-story building.[1] Indeed, we are fearfully and wonderfully made.

Yet, there is a great tragedy: people fail to use their minds. Many people stop learning after finishing school. The typical American does not read a single book during the course of a calendar year. Increasing numbers of Americans are becoming functionally illiterate. When approaching a stop light at an intersection, I was intrigued by a bumper sticker on the car in front of me which read: "If you think education is expensive, try ignorance." Indeed, a failure to use our God-given minds is a tragedy, particularly when we fail to think analytically.

Analytical thinking is a necessary skill of leaders, as it is essential in providing vision for the local church. Elders must practice the discipline of strategic, analytical thinking as they lead the local church. Yet, tragically this, often, is not the case. We fail to use our minds. Years ago, our family took a vacation to Florida and we toured the winter home of Dr. Thomas Edison in Fort Myers. While taking the tour, the guide told us that when Dr. Edison was there, he would spend hours fishing from the end of his dock. While doing so, no one was permitted to step foot on the dock, not even Mrs. Edison. The good inventor wanted to be left alone—to think. After he died, a journal entry revealed that Dr. Edison never baited the fish hook as he didn't want the fish to bother him. He simply wanted to use his mind to think analytically. Could that be why Edison became one of the most prolific inventors of our nation?

What if we were to use our minds to the same degree in thinking strategically? Could we lead the local church to be far more effectively ?

↩ **Reflection Question:** When has your eldership ever set aside a time simply to brainstorm? Share ideas, assess them, and plan for the future? Is such an activity regarded as a burden, a necessary evil, or an opportunity for improvement?

The Bible and Analytical Thinking

Numerous examples of analytical thinking can be found in Scripture. Leaders practiced this discipline in the course of their walk with God. In Acts 6:1-7, the apostles admitted there was a burgeoning problem in the first-century church in Jerusalem. The Greek-speaking widows were being overlooked in the daily distribution of food. The tense used in the original language indicates that this was not a first time occurrence (verse 1). It had happened before. So, the leaders practiced analytical thinking. They devised a plan that would solve their dilemma, and as a result, the word of God spread and more people became obedient to the faith—including a large number of priests (verse 7). Would that have happened if the leaders failed to think strategically? Probably not. Leaders in the early Church were determined to lead effectively, and that required them to think analytically.

Another example is seen in the life of Nehemiah (see Nehemiah 2:11-18). When he returned to Jerusalem to rebuild the city walls, he examined the debris field at night. Interesting. Why at night? Why not during the day when the sun would be bright and he would be able to see clearly? Simply put, Nehemiah wanted to be left alone—to think analytically. When the sun went down, people went into their homes, clearing the streets and closing their shops. People went to bed at night. So, Nehemiah would have been left alone to think strategically, seeing what he was up against in the rebuilding of the walls.

Moses sent the spies into Canaan to see what they were up against (see Numbers 13:1-25). The spies were to examine the land: its topography and agriculture. They were to study the people sociologically. For forty days, they were to make observations about the land they were soon to enter. They had to use their minds, thinking analytically and strategically.

Not only are there examples of leaders practicing the discipline of analytical thinking, but there is an expectation of Jesus for us to use our minds. Notice what is similar about each of the following verses:

> When Peter came into the house, Jesus was the first to speak. "What do you think, Simon?" he asked. "From whom do the kings of the earth collect duty and taxes—from their own sons or from others?" (Matthew 17:25)

> "What do you think? If a man owns a hundred sheep, and one of them wanders away, will he not leave the ninety-nine on the hills and go to look for the one that wandered off? (Matthew 18:12)

"What do you think? There was a man who had two sons. He went to the first and said, 'Son, go and work today in the vineyard.'" (Matthew 21:28)

"What do you think about the Christ? Whose son is he?" (Matthew 22:42)

Do you hear and see the recurring question? Four times, Jesus posed the question, "What do you think?" There is a rule in hermeneutics (i.e., the science of biblical interpretation) that when something is repeated, it is important. When something repeats in the text, God attempts to get our attention with that particular word or phrase. So, in this instance, when Jesus repeatedly asked, "What do you think," He infers that we are to use our minds! Again, we have been fearfully and wonderfully made, and we are to use our God-given minds to think more deeply. Jesus wants us to think.

In 1 Chronicles 12:32, we read that the sons of Issachar were men who had minds to understand the times and they knew what Israel should do. The context of this verse is full of insight. King Saul was no longer leading Israel. He had committed suicide in battle, and David was now king. The nation of Israel was at a defining moment,  and there were men who were skilled at reading their culture and they knew how to respond as a nation. In the same manner, these are defining days for the American Church, and we need leaders who have minds to understand the times and know how the local church should then respond. Such thinking is analytical in nature.

Day after day, we drive in and around our neighborhoods going to and from work, running errands, and more. In the same manner, we drive through the neighborhoods surrounding the church campus of which we are leaders. While doing so, we typically have a myriad of things on our minds, and we fail to notice what is going on around us. Our minds are pulled in many different directions, and our thoughts are shallow, at best.

Yet, to be effective leaders, we need to observe what is happening all around us. Analytical thinking demands that we do some "looking around" in a focused manner at what is happening in our neighborhood, our community, our state, and even across our country (i.e., the culture). The practice of "looking around" involves asking the following seven questions. By asking these questions periodically, the practice helps us to develop "minds that understand the times so that we know what the local church should do".

⮞ Question 1: What is happening culturally?

Study the population around the church. Are a significant number of people of the same generation? What are some of the demographic traits about the population: average level of education, income, family size, home size, etc.? Is the population increasing, decreasing or stagnant? Is there evidence of multiple ethnicities? For example, in a five mile radius of The Creek, over 70% of the population is married with children. So, we make a significant investment in our youth and family ministry areas. Only one out of four individuals has completed a college degree. As a result, people can complete a bachelor or master's degree at The Creek through Cincinnati Christian University. We've completed door-to-door surveys of our community to determine what concerns them, and they responded with marriage and family issues, desire for financial security, and hope for retire someday. Hence, we've implemented marriage enrichment and personal financial training opportunities. Look at your culture, analyze how the population is changing, and respond accordingly. Consider using The Percept Group for obtaining demographic information about your community (www.perceptgroup.com), as they have provided ministry based information for over twenty years to church leaders. The Percept Group knows what you need to know about the neighborhood surrounding your campus.

Reflection Question: How would you describe the community in which you are located? Even broader, what is the culture of the community in which you serve? What might they say about your congregation? How does your congregation "connect" to that culture? What cultural barriers does your church present to someone visiting the congregation?

Question 2: What is happening technologically?

Technology is rapidly changing, and it is essential that the local church make use of technology for advancing the kingdom. If there is little or no evidence of technology, people will view the local church as being irrelevant and out of touch with the culture. Using technology, leaders can survey the congregation and community for helpful information. Electronic communication can move in the local church further away from the print media and into a paperless environment. E-newsletters and invitations to activities at the church can save kingdom resources from being spent on printing and postage. Technology can be used for the teaching of classes. Colleges use on-line learning environments for many of their basic courses. Likewise, the local church can begin to offer entry level Bible studies on-line for individuals. Consider using video on the church website for promoting a program, providing a tour of the campus, or podcasting a service. Provide free downloads of sermons and lessons. Technology is a great tool for advancing the kingdom of God.

Question 3: What is happening educationally?

When thinking analytically about your community, you must give consideration to education. Regretfully, fewer people are pursuing education and it appears that a dumbing-down of America is indeed happening. Fewer people read and write. Growing numbers of high school graduates cannot read their high school diploma, while increasing numbers of Americans are functionally or marginally illiterate. If that is true in your community, how does that impact your local church ministry? What words are you using in power point displays, or in the delivery of sermons and lessons? Are they understood by the people present? As well, how are you stretching the people to a higher level of understanding in the Word of God?

Question 4: What is happening economically?

Thinking analytically mandates that we look at the economic health of our community. What is the unemployment rate? Is there evidence of businesses opening or closing? What's the foreclosure rate in the neighborhood surrounding the church? Knowing the state of the economy can impact decisions such as whether or not to embark on a capital campaign. The Creek has deliberately moved into a cash-only era. We designed a recent addition on our campus so that it could be built without incurring additional debt. As funds came available through faithful, generous giving, only then did additional work continue on the structure. We trust God to provide through the generous and faithful giving of His people, and through careful spending of the resources entrusted to the leadership.

Question 5: What is happening vocationally?

Examine the job market in your area. Are there few jobs available? Are more people being laid-off? Are people moving to other communities in hopes of finding work? Roughly 20% of the American population relocates every year, and many of the relocations are job-related. Do you spend time training and equipping people for service only to have them move from the area because of being unemployed or underemployed?

&*e* Question 6: What is happening relationally?

Relationships are changing. The family has been redefined. It is no longer biological. An entire generation has been profoundly impacted by divorce and remarriage. Grown children have felt abandoned by parents who walked out on the family. So, they have formed their "families" through friendships. The sitcom *Friends*, was a series about a group of friends who were committed to one another. This one television show helped to redefine the American family, and relationships morphed. Christians who divorce are as numerous as non-believers who are divorcing. More people are cohabiting now than ever before in the history of our nation. Many people question the need for conventional marriage, and even contend that the institution of marriage is outdated for this modern era. As well, same-sex marriage continues to be demanded as an equal right by those of the gay-lesbian community. How are relationships changing in your community?

&*e* Question 7: What is happening spiritually?

The spiritual dimension of our culture is changing dramatically, particularly in the body of Christ. American Christianity is being defined in a variety of ways as people develop their own, personalized versions of the faith. People are reluctant to commit to a specific, local church and often attend more than one church on a rotating basis. People often resist committing their financial resources to the local church, as tithing becomes less practiced. It is growing increasingly difficult to motivate people to serve in the body of Christ. Morality among believers continues to ebb. Believers know and practice little biblical doctrine in their personal lives. It is essential to ask what is happening spiritually in our congregation, our community, and our culture.

🏳 **Reflection Question:** The text provided several questions, #2-7, about culture. How would you describe these in your congregation's context? Write a brief paragraph on each, perhaps only 2-3 sentences long, so as to articulate your perspective on these elements of the culture. Also, share them in the group with others to see how your perceptions match theirs. Make a composite picture of the community, merging all your perceptions together. Now, as I have suggested, how can your congregation minister effectively in these circumstances?

When elders think analytically, they soon notice the dramatic changes that are taking place all around them. George Barna has been known to say that our culture changes every three to five years. From the way we spend our discretionary time and money to the way we dress and talk, our culture is rapidly changing. Analytical thinking points to that reality, and as a result, leaders realize their need to respond to the changing environment if the local church is to remain relevant to our spiritually lost culture. To implement change means that we must make effective decisions, and not ignore our responsibilities to lead decisively.

What would we do if we received a diagnosis of congestive heart failure because of blocked arteries? More than likely, we would follow our cardiologist's recommendation to have heart by-pass surgery. The surgeon would counsel us to change our lifestyle once we recuperate from the surgery. Fried foods and sugar-laden desserts would have to go. Vices of smoking and drinking would have to become a thing of the past. We would need to break out the sneakers and begin walking many miles. Our surgeon would warn us that if we do not change our ways, we will die. Surgery alone cannot remedy congestive heart failure. In the same manner, elders must be willing to change how they "do church" (i.e., methodology) or the local church will die. When we refuse to change, we are declaring that we would rather die than change. Regretfully, thousands of churches across America are becoming such statistics.

Effective Decision Making

So, how do we make effective decisions? Is there a model for doing so? Are there insights to embrace and follow? The first century church was faced with making a painful decision, one that needed to be made well, as much was at stake. We read of this defining moment in Acts 15, and it is known as the Jerusalem Council, when the leaders of the local church were called to exercise exceptional skill in executing change. The model of effective decision making is found in Acts 15:1-35.

Before looking at the content of a passage, we must examine its context. Contextually, there was a theological issue of great importance facing the early church. Believers were of differing opinions regarding the Gentiles. There were those who insisted that Gentiles first had to be circumcised, becoming a Jew, then they could become as Christian (see verses 1-2). This was such a volatile issue that a delegation was sent to Jerusalem to have the issue settled, both formally and finally.

Likewise, just as the early church had to deal with this volatile issue, we must deal decisively with issues facing the twenty-first century church. If we fail to think analytically, we will not be able to make decisions effectively that resolve volatile issues.

Now, let's take a look at the content of the passage. People of varying beliefs had the opportunity to present their positions. First, those belonging to the party of the Pharisees presented their belief that a Gentile had to first be circumcised before becoming a follower of Christ (Acts 15:5). These men were legalists. The "party of the Pharisees" refers to the ultra-conservative Messianic Jews. Then, Peter, Paul and Barnabas presented their position (Acts 15:6-12). Peter spoke theologically, while Paul and Barnabas spoke practically of how God was affirming the salvation of the Gentiles through miraculous signs and wonders. Notice that Acts 15:12 states, "The whole assembly became silent as they listened…" The various positions were given careful attention as people listened carefully. Finally, James said, "listen to me" (Acts 15:13), and it was of significant importance. This is an imperative (i.e., command), and this particular word occurs nowhere else in the New Testament. It is a unique word indicating that James was given both the respect and authority to lead. So, what we see happening in these opening verses of the passage is communication taking place between all parties involved, which is our first of four insights for making good decisions.

Effective decision making requires communication. There is an essential need to communicate when making decisions and executing change. Far too often, change is ineffective because communication is  ineffective. When the need for, the benefits of, the reasons behind a decision and change are not communicated, followers will resist change. Communication is essential. There are five levels of communication in our culture: 1) cliché, 2) reporting facts, 3) sharing opinions, 4) sharing feelings, and 5) complete honesty. Levels 1 and 2 are shallow and insignificant. Whereas, real communication doesn't begin until level 3, because only then do we risk being rejected by those with whom we are communicating. We must go to greater depths of communicating when entertaining a significant decision.

Referring back to the text, let's consider James, the half-brother of Jesus. Though he grew up with Jesus, he came to be a believer following the resurrection of Jesus from the dead (1 Cor. 15:7). He was also known as James, the Just—"just" because he was very Jewish in his Christianity. Becoming a Messianic Jew, James maintained his Jewish beliefs and values. Though he was very conservative in his Jewish beliefs, this text reveals that James suspended his Jewish inclinations while the two positions of belief were being presented. James, the Just, had an open mind and a teachable spirit, which reveals our second insight.

Effective decision making requires an open mind. It has been said that one of the hardest things to open is a closed mind. When faced with a significant decision, leaders must be teachable in spirit and have open minds. Far too many elders already have their minds made up regarding a decision long before coming to the discussion table. Analytical thinking requires an open mind, which leads to the effective making of decisions with open minds.

Notice also that James, the Just cited Acts 15:15-18, "The words of the prophets are in agreement with this, as it is written: 'After this I will return and rebuild David's fallen tent. Its ruins I will rebuild, and I will restore it, that the remnant of men may seek the Lord, and all the Gentiles who bear my name, says the Lord, who does these things that have been known for ages." James did not pull out the scroll of Amos and then begin reading. He simply knew the Word well enough to not only quote it, but to make a decision in keeping with it. The decision being made in this moment was made in keeping with scriptural truth.

Effective decision making requires that we follow biblical principles. Elders must be able to make decisions in keeping with biblical truth. Elders should know the Word so well that decisions affecting change will fit the paradigm of Scripture.

James, the Just saw the kingdom purpose behind this issue, calling for change. Notice his decision: "It is my judgment, therefore, that we should not make it difficult for the Gentiles who are turning to God" (Acts 15:19). James was concerned for the spiritual well-being of the lost. He knew that the mission of the church was to bring lost people to Christ. As a leader, he was fully committed to the purpose of the church, and made a decision in light of that purpose.

Effective decision making requires that we remain committed to our purpose. Our primary purpose is to make disciples of all people. We are to bring lost people into a saving relationship with Jesus Christ. Everything we do in the local church is secondary to this fact. Far too many of our decisions reflect a focus on what we want and desire. We make decisions about times of services, styles of worship, programming activities, etc. that please us; decisions that have little or no appeal to those outside of Christ.

So, to make effective decisions, we must 1) communicate, 2) have open minds, 3) follow biblical principles, and 4) remain committed to our primary purpose. If we follow this model in the making of decisions, we will be effective in making changes that are appropriate in light of our analytical thinking. In this way, we have minds to understand the times and know what the local church should do in response to our culture. Strong decision-making, followed by necessary and appropriate changes are the result of analytical thinking. They go hand in hand.

Reflection Question: How often does the eldership engage in intentional Bible study when addressing the work of the church? How is Scripture used in the decision making process? If it is not, then upon what are decisions being made?

Reasons for Resisting Change

Many people are resist change. In spite of how well educated we are or how open-minded we may think we are, we still resist change. The following is the "ten-top list" of reasons as to why people resist change.

(1) The change was not self-initiated. People feel manipulated and lack ownership in the decision being made.

(2) Routine is disrupted. People like their routines. For example, if a change is made in the worship schedule, some will resist the change because it changes their Sunday morning routine.

(3) Change creates fear of the unknown. People do not like insecurity.

(4) Change creates fear of failure. People like success, and in particular, the success of their church.

(5) The purpose of the change is unclear. This is a result of poor communication occurring.

(6) People like to keep things the way they are. People like status quo and traditions, even if it means the spiritually lost are not reached with new, relevant methods.

(7) The rewards for change do not match the effort change requires. People feel that change is not worth the effort if the rewards are not immediate and significant.

(8) Negative thinking prevails. The "can't, won't and don't mentality" reigns in the minds of people.

(9) There is a lack of respect and trust in leadership. Prior mistakes and misjudgments made by the leaders cause people to resist change being proposed by the leadership.

(10) Change requires additional commitment. People resist change because it will cost them personally in some way, such as in making a greater effort in implementing the change.

Reflection Question: Given these ten common resistors to change, in the space provided below please rank in order (highest to lowest) your own personal resistors to change. Which ones most apply to you to those that least applies to you?

Rank	Resistor	Comment/Explanation
1		
2		
3		
4		
5		
6		
7		
8		
9		
10		

Once finished, share your responses as an eldership. Be aware of those resistors that a large number of elders share in common, since this would drastically effect how decisions are made and strategic planning is done.

Creating a Climate for Change

To counter resistance to change, it is essential to create an environment in which change is welcomed and embraced. Studies have shown that people do not resist change so much as they resist being changed! In order for changes to occur effectively, a healthy climate or environment must be created within the organization and among the people. Elders can create such an environment by pursuing these four initiatives.

First, develop a trust with the people. Building trust requires time. The longer you serve with consistent effectiveness, the greater trust is built among people. Trust in leadership creates a climate in which change can be made.

Second, leaders must set the example. People need to see the elders making personal effort in executing change, no matter the cost. We lead by example. The Apostle Paul said to follow his example as he followed the example of Christ (1 Cor. 11:1).

Third, leaders must understand the history of the local church. Change for the future can be made only when we have an appreciation for what happened in the past. Acknowledging and respecting the efforts of people in previous years helps to create a climate for change.

Finally, leaders must be able to influence others in a positive way. When inviting others along to "take the hill together", a climate is created that embraces change.

☚ Reflection Question: A Check List for Change

When making decisions that introduce change in the local church, proper timing for implementing the change becomes an issue. There are right and wrong times for implementing changes. Review the following questions located on the next page before implementing a proposed change. By doing so, you can determine if now is the right time for the change—or not. When the questions are answered with "yes," the change tends to be easier. Questions that are answered with "no" usually indicate that the change will be difficult, and perhaps, a bit premature.

YES	NO	
☐	☐	Will this change benefit the local church?
☐	☐	Is this change compatible with the purpose of the church?
☐	☐	Is this change specific and clear?
☐	☐	Are the influential people in favor of the change?
☐	☐	Is it possible to test this change before making it permanent?
☐	☐	Is this change reversible?
☐	☐	Are all the resources available to make this change?
☐	☐	Is this change the next obvious step?
☐	☐	Does this change have both short and long range benefits?
☐	☐	Is the leadership capable of bringing about this change?
☐	☐	Is the timing right?

Jon Krakauer made the summit of Mt. Everest on May10, 1996, and told of that harrowing experience in his book *Into Thin Air*. Making it to the summit, Krakauer paused only for a few moments before beginning his descent as he was physically exhausted and oxygen deprived. While descending, he became enveloped by some clouds, and it was not long before lightning, thunder and snow began to disorient him. Fortunately, he was able to make it to Base Camp Four before the full fury of a storm covered the summit.

Four climbers made it to the summit after Krakauer and did not have ample time to make it to Base Camp Four before darkness.

The storm caused them to lose their way, and being exhausted, they laid down to wait out the storm. When morning came, they found that they had laid down just one step away from the precipice of the south wall of Everest. They slept through the darkness and blinding snow on the edge of a cliff—one step away from death!

The dark wind of our culture is blinding us as leaders of the local church. Far too many of us are spiritually asleep and just one step away from calamity. The darkness of skepticism and winds of apathy cause us to lie down in lethargy. It is essential that we wake up, think analytically and make effective decisions that are right responses for the local church.

"The sons of Issachar were men who understood the times
and knew what Israel should do."
1 Chronicles 12:32

Endnotes

[1] http://www.pbc.org/files/messages/11585/0280.html

Chapter 3

Looking Ahead: Leading Through Strategic Planning

Gary L. Johnson

"Leadership is accepting people where they are,
then taking them somewhere."
C.W. Perry

The State of the American Church

Why is it that guys typically do not like to go to the doctor? We would rather tough it through an illness than go see the doctor. We tend to think that whatever our illness is, we'll just work through it and it will eventually go away. We tend to live in a state of denial when it comes to our health, particularly as it declines as we age. Sadly, we behave in much the same way as leaders of the local church. If something is wrong in the body of Christ, we tend to be passive leaders—believing that the issue or problem will just work itself out and go away. Yet, the body of Christ is in serious condition, and we can no longer live in a state of denial.

Simply put, the American Church is in decline. Mainline denominations have been declining for decades. Evangelical churches have lost their voice, and are losing their influence upon our culture. The Roman Catholic Church is in a crisis due to a priest shortage and sex scandal. Typically, we hear that four out of ten Americans are in church on any given Sunday. Yet, this is far from accurate. David T. Olson, director of the American Church Research Project and author of *The American Church in Crisis*, has completed an extensive study of church attendance in over 200,000 churches, and it revealed a dramatic decrease in the number of Americans attending church, with only 17.5% of Americans attending church in 2005. If the present trend continues, church attendance in 2050 is estimated to be 10% or less.[1] Three times as many churches are closing annually (3500-4000) compared to the number being planted (1300-1500).[2] It is estimated that 85% of churches have reached a plateau or are declining. The Associated Press (9/26/09) reported a "dramatic increase in Americans declaring no religion", up from 14 million Americans in 1990 to 34 million Americans in 2008, and the number continues to rise with every passing year.

The American Church is in decline. Why? Could the failure of the American Church be due to a failure in leadership? There is a premise that states an organization can rise to a level of greatness equal to that of the level of leadership within the organization. Could it be that the American Church has failed to advance the kingdom of God because leaders are failing to move the local church forward? God designed His Church to move forward, advancing His purposes around the world, throughout the ages. Leaders move people forward.

Reflection Question: Reflect on your own congregation over the past ten years. Has attendance increased or decreased (look at the numbers, not your perceptions)? How many individuals are you adding to your congregation annually? Are they from conversions outside the church, or additions from families within the church; baptism or transfers? Is your church a declining, plateaued, or ascending congregation?

Forward–Thinking is Biblical Thinking

One of the most effective leaders in the early church was the Apostle Paul. While imprisoned, Paul wrote a moving letter to the Church in Philippi, and in the letter, Paul made a startling comment: "But one thing I do: Forgetting what is behind and straining toward what is ahead, I press on toward the goal to win the prize for which

God has called me heavenward in Christ Jesus. All of us who are mature should take such a view of things" (Phil. 3:13-15).

Paul did not live in the past. He did not dwell on his many previous accomplishments, nor was he consumed with his many problems. Paul made it a practice to be forward in his thinking. He thought about life in eternity with Christ. He thought about the tomorrows of life. Moreover, Paul said that those who are spiritually mature should take such a view of things.

Elders are assumed to be the spiritually mature leaders of the local church, and being mature, they should be forward in their thinking. Elders should not be dwelling on the past history of the local church, whether pleasant or painful in nature. Elders need to be thinking about the future of the local church—specifically, how to move the local church forward in advancing the kingdom of God. Leaders move people forward.

Australia has a most interesting coat of arms. It depicts two creatures that are unique to their nation: the kangaroo and the emu. These two creatures share a common trait—one that appeals to the people of Australia. An emu is a flightless bird with three-toed feet, and can only move forward. A kangaroo has a sizeable tail, which prevents it from moving backward. Both creatures can only move in a forward direction, and the Australian coat of arms declares that spirit as belonging to their nation; a nation that only moves forward in spirit and action. The Church must move forward, and moving the Church forward is the responsibility of the leadership.

Reflection Question: Review the last six months of elder's meeting minutes. Listen for the tone of the meeting. Is it more future focused, planning ahead, sharing and enacting vision; or is it more past focused, reactive to events that have already occurred?

Future Trends Facing the American Church

It is essential for elders to be forward in their thinking, as the American Church is facing changes unlike anything in the past. Alan Nelson, executive editor of *Rev!* Magazine, wrote an article highlighting twelve trends facing the American Church over the next ten years.[3] These trends are of significant importance, and they are impacting the local church now. If we do not begin to think in a forward manner, we will fail to move people forward and ministry in the local church will become highly irrelevant.

From his list of twelve trends, Nelson points out that there will be fewer mega-campuses, but more mega-ministries. With advancing technologies, large mega-campuses will not be needed. Younger people are not compelled to build large worship complexes. Multi-sites venues will continue to grow in popularity. The ever-popular Starbucks do not have shops with seating for hundreds, but they do have multiple locations in close proximity to one another.

The trend of a diminishing Christian orientation will continue. As mentioned earlier, only 17% of Americans go to church on any given Sunday, and the decline will continue. Religious pluralism is expanding in our culture, particularly with an increase of people calling for a freedom from religion. The atheistic and agnostic movements are growing on university and college campuses, as well as in larger metropolitan areas.

Nelson listed other trends of importance: a movement towards being simple, with a focus on mission; discipleship and outreach will happen through service opportunities, such as short term mission trips; house churches will continue to morph; growing ethnic diversity will be present; decentralized training must happen, particularly through use of technology; mergers and transfer of physical assets will happen with the closing of thousands of churches; family ministry will be emphasized just as youth ministry was since the 70s; and, America will not be "Christian central" in the world.

Between now and 2018, the American Church will change in both appearance and activity. As leaders, are we forward in our thinking so that we can anticipate this change? Elders are to determine where the Church is headed, which is no easy task, but it is an essential task. It's time for elders to practice strategic planning.

Common Myths of Strategic Planning

Far too many elders fail to do strategic planning because of buying into the following myths associated with strategic planning. The first myth states that strategic planning is only for large churches. On the contrary, when churches practice this discipline, they are prone to grow. Strategic planning helps to foster an environment of growth.

A second myth states that strategic planning will split the church. Yet, planning can—and does—draw people together in a spirit of unity. With the local church moving in one primary direction, people are drawn together. Those individuals who do not support the leadership direction provided by the elders, can—and may—cease to attend the local church. Strategic planning helps to create a stronger, healthier unity.

A third myth states that strategic planning is a function of only the leaders of the church. However, when strategic planning is done effectively, it can—and should—involve a broad representation of the congregation.

A fourth myth states that strategic planning should be "hired out" to professional consultants. Do not shirk the responsibility of practicing periodic strategic planning by transferring this task to church consultants. You can engage such a professional to help you produce your first strategic plan, and the local church can also be benefitted by their objective observations. But, at some point in time, the leadership of the local church must realize that both the capability and responsibility for this task lies with them. People in the local church know their congregation and the history of the church far better than anyone else. By drawing on the insights and involving the skills of people in the local church, a strategic plan can be both produced by and owned by the people.

Reflection Question: Which of these four myths is most prevalent in your eldership? Which one do you most readily espouse? Can you think of an instance it has impacted the decision making and planning of the eldership?

Direct Benefits of Strategic Planning

Just as common myths are associated with strategic planning, direct benefits also accompany this discipline.

First, strategic planning provides a sense of direction and purpose. A long range plan enables the local church to have a focused, future target. Far too many churches exist from week to week. Little thought is given to where the local church is headed beyond the next approaching Sunday.

Second, strategic planning helps with the wise use of resources. The recession of 2008-09 has had a significant impact on churches and para-church ministries. Resources once stretched thin, are now all the more scarce. Strategic planning helps to make the wisest use of these resources as purpose and priorities are now identified.

Third, strategic planning is evangelistic. Time is the most expensive non-renewable commodity in our culture. People are possessive of their time, and they will not invest their time in what appears to be irrelevant organizations. People are drawn to a church that seems to have momentum, an energetic movement forward. People want to be a part of a vital church that is going somewhere significant.

Lastly, strategic planning reduces the trauma caused by changes in leadership. When an effective, long-term minister retires or resigns from the local church, the congregation can flounder. Yet, when a vision has been developed and is "owned" by the congregation, there is less trauma in the congregation when leadership changes occur. A written strategic plan provides the church with specific direction, and this plan "outlives" individual leaders.

Working Definition of Vision

Simply put, vision is a picture of the future that produces excitement within you. In 1774, John Adams spoke of a new nation--a union of 13 states--being born--a nation dependent from the Parliament and separate from England. That picture produced excitement in the lives of people, who worked sacrificially to make it become a reality. Shortly after the turn of the century, Henry Ford envisioned automobiles affordable for every American family. Though he was ridiculed by many for such an outlandish idea, his vision became reality with millions of Model-Ts were produced and purchased by the American people. In the 1940s, Billy Graham said that someday there would be evangelistic crusades in stadiums across our nation and around the world. Again, that vision produced excitement in the lives of people and a dream came true. Over two hundred million people have gathered for Billy Graham crusades and over one billion have watched via television.

Vision is a picture of the future that produces excitement within you—and others. Are people excited about the future in the local church you lead? If not, why not? Could it be that there is not a succinct, God-honoring vision even within the minds of leaders? Remember, leaders are to move people forward.

Reflection Question: If someone were to ask, "What is the mission of our congregation and how are we trying to achieve it?" How well could the answer be articulated? Would everyone in the congregation know it? How viable is your congregation's sense of vision?

Knowing When to Develop a Strategic Plan

There are specific times when strategic planning should and must take place. Moses cast a vision for taking the Promised Land prior to his death. King David cast a vision for the building of the Temple prior to his death. Even Jesus Christ cast a vision for "making disciples of all nations" prior to ascending into heaven. The following questions can help determine if now is the time for you to craft a strategic plan for the church you lead. [*These questions can serve as reflection questions for this section, and can be answered first individually and then shared with one another in a retreat or development session.*]

(1) What is the "state of the church?" Are you growing numerically? Are people being converted to Christianity and is there actual evidence that lives are being transformed into the likeness of Christ? Have you reached a plateau?

(2) Have you brought closure to the history of the church? Have you mourned failures from the past? Celebrated victories? Reconciled differences?

(3) Have you developed a mission or vision statement? Is it known? Is it visible? Is it "owned" by the people?

(4) Have you identified the core values of the church? Do you see these as being non-negotiable to the congregation?

(5) Is the Holy Spirit moving on the hearts of leaders to spur the people forward?

Six Steps of Strategic Planning

The following are six simple steps to follow in order to complete a long range plan for the local church. The word "simple" is used in that the local church can pursue this task without hiring professional consultants. On the other hand, this process—when done thoroughly and well—will take considerable time. Each successive strategic plan that you develop and use becomes easier as a process.

➤ Step #1: Lay the Ground Work

Make certain that the vision or mission statement for the local church is in place. The statement should be 1) short—so that it can be known and memorized; 2) specific, so that it can be measured; and 3) scriptural, so that it is a reflection of truth.

The Creek has a vision statement of "Transforming lives…one at a time." It is widely known by people of all ages in our congregation. It is measurable in that people can state how the Lord has transformed their lives here. It is a reflection of Scripture (i.e., Rom. 12:2, 2 Cor. 5:17).

Laying the ground work also requires that core values be established by the leaders of the church. Elders and key staff establish the values. Core values are like the operating system of a computer in that decisions are made by leadership in keeping with the core values. Once the core values have been established, publish them, preach and teach them, and most importantly—use them in the making of decisions. Also, make the core values rank ordered so that one leads to the next.

For example, The Creek faced a need for additional facilities. The first set of blueprints estimated a construction cost of $13 million, but because our fourth core value states that we are faithful stewards, we scrapped those plans and went back to the drawing board. A non-adorned, functional complex was built for $5.5 million and with cash so that we did not pass increasing debt to the next generation of believers. Core values are to be used. For a listing of our five rank

ordered   core   values,   please   visit   www.thecreek.org/
missionvisionvalues.

➢ Step #2: Form the Team

The elders should appoint a team of individuals, and delegate to them the responsibility of developing a strategic plan for the church. Representatives from among the elders should be a part of the team so that elder involvement happens. The "Dream Team" should be a cross section of people in the church, and each of them should have a desire to serve in this project, as well as having competencies for doing so. People involved in strategic planning should be people of Christian character and commitment.

The leader of the "Dream Team" should be the senior minister since he will communicate the strategic plan to the church, casting the vision for people to pursue. He should be the one to coordinate the development of the plan. A victory will be achieved only when everyone is working together, and this team needs a voice to follow. Winston Churchill said, "The nation had the lion's heart. I had the luck to give the roar."

The "Dream Team" is made up of smaller, specific teams. Determine what the major ministry areas exist in your congregation (i.e., evangelism, missions, discipleship, administration, worship, children, student ministry, etc.). Each of these areas is to be a smaller team, and each of them should be meeting to develop a plan for its area of responsibility. These smaller teams must meet separately, and be led by either a staff member over the area or by a skilled volunteer leader already serving in that ministry area. These smaller teams should be made up of four to five individuals. Each of the leaders of these smaller teams should meet with the senior minister to compile and collate the individual plans into one.

➤ **Step #3: Paint a Picture** (of the future)

Describe what the church is like by a specific time in the future. This is called a statement of preferred future. Verbalize what you picture the church to be at a specific point in the future. For example, "On this first day of (insert year), First Christian Church is a multi-ethnic church of 1,000 meeting in three worship services, etc."). The statement of preferred future should be brief—perhaps limited to as few as five sentences—and it should clearly mention the date when the strategic plan expires. The elders and key ministry leaders must write this statement that describes what the local church has become at the conclusion of the strategic plan.

For example, a recent—and measurable—statement of preferred future at the Creek reads: As we stand here on (insert future date), we see confirmation that Jesus is indeed transforming lives at The Creek. This is witnessed in our genuine worship of the living God, as growing numbers of people are drawn into an irresistible environment of adoration and praise. By strategically developing Christian leaders our increasing spheres of influence enable us to have greater spiritual impact, both locally and globally. The Creek has transitioned into a "mission-driven" culture where a greater percentage of our members are equipped and empowered to passionately serve God according to His gifting and calling. Connecting in authentic community, we are living the biblical imperatives to "love one another," "forgive one another," "encourage one another"…

It is essential during this step to determine a time span for your strategic plan. At The Creek, we tend to work in three year increments. Our culture re-invents itself every three to five years. So, the plan cannot be so long in years that it cannot be responsive to the morphing of our culture. Also, when we consider that Jesus completed His ministry in three years, it causes us to ask ourselves: What if we only had three years to accomplish what we have been given to do in our ministry? What would have to change now in order to accomplish our objectives within three years? Perhaps a three-year plan would be most ideal for your first written strategic plan because your leadership team would have to lead all the more effectively.

➢ Step #4: Develop the Plan

Using the statement of preferred future from the elders and key ministry leaders, begin to develop the strategic plan, step by step. Looking at the end-product (i.e., what the church is to resemble in the statement of preferred future), begin to set goals working backwards from that statement. Think: in order to become "this" at the end of the plan, we have to step back and accomplish "this" step by step to take us achieve the end product. Remember, the plan is to be coordinated between the various areas of ministry, and in writing. Moreover, the goals and objectives must reflect the nature of the overall mission/vision statement of the church, and help to make that mission/vision become reality. A word of caution is necessary here. Make every effort to keep the plan as simple as possible. Stating hundreds of goals and objectives will be far less effective than clearly stating far fewer, primary goals that can be both remembered and pursued.

With that in mind, the strategic planning team may want to use exercises that are a part of what is known as the Tom Paterson Process (see www.patersoncenter.com).   Developed by management con-sultant Tom Paterson, this process of strategic planning is both highly effective and interactive.   After a successful career in corporate planning with companies such as RCA, IBM, and Douglas Aircraft, Tom Paterson developed his trade-mark method of asking specific questions that move a strategic planning team through six phases:

(1) Gaining perspective by asking, "Where are we now?"

(2) Doing planning by asking, "Where are we headed?"
(3) Taking action by asking, "What is important now?"
(4) Developing structure by asking, "What is right for us now?"
(5) Managing the plan by asking, "How are we doing?"
(6) Pursuing renewal by asking, "What must change?"

These questions help move the strategic planning team through the process of developing the actual plan.

➤ Step #5: "Kick-Off" the Plan

Once completed, introduce the long range plan to the congregation. Consider having a special worship service during which to launch the plan. Be sure to express thanks to the many volunteers who invested time and energy to produce the plan. Place a printed copy in the hands of the people. Place a digital copy of the plan on the church website. Pray over the plan and dedicate its pursuit to the Lord.

Anticipate some defectors. When the twelve tribes were to move into the Promised Land, two and a half tribes wanted nothing to do with this "strategic plan" (see Joshua 14:3). Just as there were defectors among the Israelites, there will be defectors in the local church who do not want any part of such a strategic movement forward. Yet, you must stay the course. Do not allow divisive people to derail your strategic plan.

➤ Step #6: Manage the Plan

Once in place, the strategic plan must be managed. There are three specific tasks in doing so. First, mention the plan. Keep it in the forefront of the people. Keep referring to the long range plan. Second, monitor the plan to see if the goals are being pursued, and met. If not, ask why the goals are not being met. Third, modify the plan—if necessary. Events such as 9-11 derailed the strategic plans of many organizations. Remember, the plan is not set in concrete or steel. It is a flexible document, much like a budget that can be modified if necessary. When people take a vacation trip, they sometimes have to take a detour because of construction ahead or an accident has happened. Still, after making the detour, the family still arrives at their final destination. The strategic plan of the church may involve such a modification, and still arrive with the statement of preferred future becoming a reality.

Reflection Question: Rate on a scale of 1-5 (1 being low, 5 being high) your congregation's current state of strategic planning.

Item	Rank	Comment
Lay the Groundwork	① ② ③ ④ ⑤	
Form a Team	① ② ③ ④ ⑤	
Paint a Picture	① ② ③ ④ ⑤	
Develop the Plan	① ② ③ ④ ⑤	
"Kick-off" the Plan	① ② ③ ④ ⑤	
Manage the Plan	① ② ③ ④ ⑤	

Final Challenge

One of the greatest players in professional ice hockey was Wayne Gretzky. When interviewed, he was asked what made him such a stand-out, remarkable athlete in the game of hockey. Gretzky's answer was short and to the point. He said that other players skate to where the puck is, but he skated to where the puck was going.

There is a subtle difference between good leadership and exceptional leadership in the local church. Good leaders are dependable and committed, yet they tend to follow where the American Church is headed. Exceptional leaders, on the other hand, lead the local church to where she should be headed. G.K. Chesterton, one of the most influential English writers of the 20th

---

 RECOMMENDED READING:
Aubrey Malphurs; Advanced Strategic Planning (Baker Books, 1999)
Andy Stanley; Visioneering (Multnomah, 1999)

---

century, once said: "We do not want, as the newspapers say, a church that will move with the world. We want a church that will move the world." That will require elders to move people forward.

Endnotes

[1] www.americanchurch.org
[2] www.sharperiron.org/ten reasons for church planting
[3] http://www.rev.org/article.asp?ID=2820

Chapter 4

Taking under Wing: Leading by Mentoring

David Roadcup

"The things which you have heard from me in the presence of many
witnesses, entrust these to faithful men who will
be able to teach others also." (2 Tim. 2:2)

"Max Lucado sat at an elegant dinner beside a man from
Germany. To make conversation, Max asked the German gentleman
what he did for a living. The German responded, 'I am a keeper of
the forest.' 'Oh', probed Max, 'and what does a keeper of the forest
do?' 'Put simply,' the gentleman responded, "I harvest the trees my
father planted. And I plant the trees my sons will harvest. So I must
always plant more trees than I harvest.'"[1]

Putting the ideas of "elders" and "mentoring" together is an
exciting venture!

"What can we do to ensure that men will be stepping up in the
future to lead and care for our churches?" "How can we make sure
that the elders of our congregations are spiritually mature men, full of
integrity, with a heart for the gospel and the lost?" "What kind of
training can be offered to teach and develop quality elders for present
and future service?" These questions and others need to be
considered by elders and staff ministers as we look at the future of the
church and her effectiveness in winning our culture and world to
Christ.

Out of all the methods available today to equip and train
people for leadership, one of the most effective means for producing
quality results is *the mentoring relationship* (also called "discipling").
Developing mentoring relationships between our present elders,

ministers and men who are potential elders is one of the most effective ways to assure quality leadership for the church in the coming years.

This chapter is a plea to every elder (and staff member) to be growing spiritually themselves. Our plea is also for our present leaders to understand the need to be proactive in developing the future leadership core of the church. This relationship can powerfully stimulate growth and spiritual understanding for those who participate. Through this chapter, I am purposefully asking you as a leader in the church to consider personal participation in the ministry of mentoring. The information below will explain what mentoring is and how it is done.

☞ **Reflection Question:** Think of your own past, even back to childhood; who has served as mentors in your life? Who has left a spiritual fingerprint on your walk with Christ? Who may have had a profound influence on your life's direction and character? Now, ask yourself, have I done with for anyone else?

The Need for Mentoring among Elders

Intentional and proactive training *must be* a part of the raising up of elders in any congregation. Elders who mentor future elders are crucial to a healthy church and its future. One of the most outstanding problems in the church today is the number of leaders in very important positions who execute their roles, having experienced a very small amount of training or preparation. If I could change the leadership culture of churches across the board, it would be through the development of a serious approach to the training and preparation of elders and staff. There are few churches that have training required for their present and future elders. Most elders in most churches experience no formal training. *Their training is normally limited to watching the men who are elders before them and basically doing what they have done.*

Elders have an exciting privilege and weighty responsibility! Given to every elder of the church of Jesus Christ is a calling and mandate to direct the church with spiritual wisdom and discernment. The arrangement most churches have at present for preparing men to lead is unacceptable. We need to change the way in which we prepare men for leadership in the church! With eternity is in the balance, we need to become proactive and determine that we will formulate a plan to train and develop elders.

There are several approaches to preparing future elders. Here are just a few ideas that work now for churches and their effort to train their elders:

- There needs to be a course of study that future elders need to attend. In this course or class offered in the church, men are taught the biblical concepts dealing with what an elder is and does. Qualifications of elders from 1 Timothy and Titus need to be explained and discussed. Men should be taught the importance of growing spiritually and being on the cutting edge of spirit formation in their lives. They should be taught about prayer and total dependence on the Lord, understanding that the church is an organism and not an organization.[2] They need to know the great importance of growing and maintaining relationships with people. (This is a critical key to good eldering!). Content needs to be conveyed to men considering the ministry of the eldership. (The volumes produced by e2 Effective Elders would provide excellent content for such a class.)

- There are excellent books, CDs, articles and other information available for future elders to read and internalize. Books can be read and discussed in planned meetings. Informational-training CDs can be taken in the elder's car, SUV or truck and listened to while driving to and from work.

- Assuming elders have annual or semi-annual retreats, possible future elders can be invited to join the present elders for their retreats as the time grows closer for new elders to begin their service. (I spoke at an elder's retreat recently and was impressed to find that the elder team had invited several men whom they thought would make good elders to come to the retreat, observe and become part of the experience.)
- Elder conferences, seminars and clinics are offered on a regular basis in many areas of the country. Why not have the elder and staff team attend one or more of these conferences a year? The team could attend the conference during the day. After dinner in the evening, they could meet to debrief, discuss and apply to their lives and to the church the information they received during the day. I also know of a congregation that, when taking its staff and elders to a conference, will contact one or more of the main conference speakers or seminar leaders in advance and secure them for a lunch or dinner. They will arrange with the speaker, after the meal, to make a presentation to the team on a vital topic and then entertain questions. This is a very fruitful way to customize leader training.
- In addition to the above mentioned approaches, we would add one of the most effective ways to train present and future elders. It is through the mentoring or discipling approach. We will now discuss in detail what mentoring is, how it works and how it can be done among a team of elders and staff.

🕊️ **Reflection Question:** How many of these methods listed above do you or your eldership currently use to mentor? If none, or you don't have a mentoring ministry among the elders, which method would be the best with which to start?

The Definition and Description of Mentoring

In mentoring, the person doing the leading or influencing is normally called the "mentor" or "discipler". The person being mentored can be called the "protégé", "mentee" or "disciple". The overall process can be referred to as "mentoring", "discipling", "apprenticing" or "interning". (For this chapter, the terms "mentor", "protégé" and "mentoring" will be used.)

Mentoring is *the process of an experienced person proactively relating to, coaching, teaching, directing, encouraging and stretching a less experienced person in a particular vocation, ability or desired field of endeavor through relationship, study, time and involvement.*

Mentoring for our purposes, basically works like this: A man who has been in the Lord for a number of years, has good mental and emotional health, has experience in life and family and an acceptable level of maturity, chooses one or more men to begin meeting with and developing in matters of character, ability and/or vocation. There is a serious commitment on both the part of the mentor and protégé. The heart of the process is built on relationship.

Mentoring is teaching and coaching. The process always takes time and attention. Effective mentoring involves the stretching and challenging of the protégé by the mentor. Mentoring provides a base of support and a source of encouragement for the protégé. This process can be done one on one or the mentor can have multiple protégés in a group. If a mentor is going to work with a group, the number recommended is up to four.

The focused idea of mentoring comes down to this – an experienced person who has the ability to teach and influence proactively assists one or more persons to develop and grow in the discipline or in achieving the desired outcomes.

The History of Mentoring

The word *mentor* has an interesting background. History tells us that when the Greek warrior, Odysseus went off to fight the Trojan War, he left his youngest son, Telemachus, in the care of a trusted guardian named Mentor. The siege of Troy lasted ten years, and it took Odysseus another ten years to make his way home. When he arrived, he found that the boy, Telemachus had grown into a man, thanks to Mentor's wise tutelage."[3]

We know that the concept of mentoring was practiced by the Greeks, Romans, Jews and multitudes of other cultures. History also tells us that mentoring was the main form of vocational preparation for centuries. Margo Murray explains, "These same principles of modeling and mentoring have been key elements in the continuity of art, craft, and commerce from ancient times. A good example can be found in the craft guilds that began in the Middle Ages. These societies helped structure the professions of merchant, lawyer, goldsmith and others."[4] Jesus found this to be a preferred way to train future leaders as He called the twelve to be with Him and to learn from Him. The apostle Paul also used this method extensively. From Scriptural account, we can name his mentees/disciples (Timothy, Mark, Silas, Philemon, etc).

For ages, cultures knew that mentoring/discipling was an incredibly effective way to train and develop people. The church would advance in strength and effectiveness if she were to seriously awaken to this practice. What a benefit it would be to the church if elders and staff were to seriously consider the practice of mentoring.

The fruitfulness of the church would be significant if leaders began mentoring in a focused and proactive way! The difference it would make in the maturity levels of our church leaders and in the overall effectiveness of our churches would be awesome!

The Issue of Time and Availability in Mentoring

In today's culture, one of the most important aspects of mentoring and being mentored comes down to time, schedule and availability. With the extreme demands on our time and schedules, we must choose the issues that deserve our focus and time. Time is today's currency.

"Harold's lip quivered slightly as he wrung his napkin. He wore a gracious attempt at a smile, but his eyes revealed weariness and a bit of pain. ' 'Shepherd' is a beautiful idea,' he began, 'Looks to me like that is what God wants of me as an elder in this church. But I am feeling at a total loss. How do I actually make this happen in the real world? Why, the first three days last week I was in New York to close a contract. Then I was back in the office for two more marathon days fighting paper wars. My desk wasn't even clean till I headed for Houston to inspect a plant there. I hit the deck by 5 a.m. and run all day. Maybe last week was worse than usual, but not much. And I'm not alone. The rest of the elders in my church find life fast-paced too. What's more, most of our congregation runs the same fast-track—young mothers, graduate students, sales managers, CEOs, attorneys, and single parents forced to work two jobs. The list runs on and on. How is a shepherd to do his thing? How do you get sheep smell on you when you don't touch them—except for a handshake and some quick words in the aisle Sunday morning, a quick phone call, or a cold, impersonal email.'"[5]

The above scenario is all too real for many people who are involved in the paid and lay leadership of a church. Our schedules are full to overflowing. Our datebooks are full of family responsibilities, appointments, meetings, assignments and deadlines at work. There are social commitments - not to mention the part that sports, hobbies, travel and other interests play in our lives. In light of what we face with our schedules each week, can we find time to participate in a mentoring relationship?

The possibility of being in a mentoring relationship comes down to one issue – *the issue* of *priorities*. A good definition of the concept of priority is simply, *the ranking of that which is important*. We decide by the level of importance what gets our time and attention and what will have to wait. Multiple needs cry out for our time, focus and energy. We must personally give attention to the fact that we only have so much time to invest and it should be invested wisely in light of the greatest return. In a very proactive manner, we must ask ourselves the following key questions:

- *"In light of my life's direction and personal goals, which of the demands on my time and personal activities are the most important?"*
- *"How do I correctly rank them?"*
- *"How does God want me to deal with this issue? What does He want me to do?"*

There is a powerful story found in Luke 10:38-42. Jesus and His disciples are lodging at the home of His good friends, Mary and Martha. Martha is busily preparing dinner but Mary is sitting at the feet of Jesus listening to Him teach. In her frustration, Martha comes to Jesus and insists that Mary help her with the preparations. Jesus response: "Martha, Martha, you are worried and bothered about so many things; *but only one thing is necessary*, for Mary has chosen the good part, which shall not be taken away from her." The one thing that Jesus mentions here is the fact that Mary was seeking Jesus and His teachings. She wanted to draw closer to the Lord. Jesus communicates here that the *one grand priority* in our lives as believers (especially leaders) is to seek Him with all of our hearts. This should be our ultimate and grand priority. There are many other very important things on our schedules, but in light of ranking that which is important, we must see that seeking the Lord and His will and Kingdom should be our most important priority. If this is so, then the arrangement of our schedule should include a time specifically dedicated to growing personally in our spiritual lives. It should also include time dedicated to helping others to grow, as well. The tyranny of the urgent will call to us over and over again. But keeping our focus clear as to what really matters and translating that priority into our personal calendars is crucial. We need to be willing to adjust our schedules and list of activities in such a way that mentoring relationships could become a serious part of our lives. It might mean saying "no" to new opportunities which are coming our way. It might mean a change by saying "no" to things which we already have on our radar. But in light of the great benefits of mentoring, the outcome would be worth the effort.

For Elders *Waiting* to be Mentored

Finding a mentor for an elder or staff member who desires to move forward in his spiritual life, family life and work is of utmost importance. A man with vast experience in mentoring states, "Where can I find someone with a little more wisdom and experience than I have who would be willing to help me as I navigate my way though life?"[6] If you sense this need, proactively initiating steps to start the process of finding someone to work with you is key. Howard Hendricks states, ".....you must deliberately and strategically place yourself in the path of opportunity, where you can increase your chances of linking up with a person who can influence you."[7] Below is a suggested plan to help you get started.

Step 1

Begin praying for the Lord to lead you to someone with whom you have chemistry and the possibility of a relationship. Ask the Lord to bring a person to mind that you could approach about mentoring. Don't be afraid to be vigilant about this. If no one immediately surfaces, give the Lord time and continue to ask. The Lord has perfect timing and knows who could be brought into your life in the capacity of mentor. Why not let Him guide you as you look for someone with whom to work?

Step 2

Look for a person with key characteristics. Howard Hendricks, one of the premier mentors and disciplers of today lists the Ten Marks of a Mentor:

(1) Seems to have what you personally need.
(2) Cultivates relationships.
(3) Is willing to take a chance on you.
(4) Is respected by other Christians.
(5) Has a network of resources.
(6) Is consulted by others.
(7) Both talks and listens.
(8) Is consistent in his lifestyle.
(9) Is able to diagnose your needs.
(10)   Is concerned with your interests.[8]

Remember, mentors do not have to be spectacular to be of great benefit to you. They just need to be solid, spiritual men who can add to and build into your life. There are many "giants" in the church who are mature, committed, God-loving believers who have the ability to make a difference in your walk with Christ and life.

Where do you find the person who could be your mentor? Here are a few suggestions:

- Is there a seasoned veteran elder or other lay person in your church whom you feel you could approach?
- Is there a staff member serving at your church that would take the time for this relationship?
- Is there a Christian college or seminary near you where you could connect with a faculty member, administrator or staff member?
- How about at work? Is there a mentor there (a colleague, supervisor, salesman or vendor) who might be a solid believer that you could approach?
- Someone you might know through social contacts? Anyone in your golf or softball league who might be a candidate?
- How about a person from another church in your area? It might be someone you have met through involvement in your church camp board or other area of ministry.
- Are there any retired ministers who live in your area? (There is an excellent Christian retirement development near the university where I teach that has many outstanding, qualified retired ministers who are still very active and involved. One of them might be available and interested.)

Step 3

Approach the person and discuss the possibilities. It is suggested that you invite a potential mentor out for breakfast or lunch to discuss the possibility of a relationship. Is this person interested? Are they available? Will they be willing to set aside the time and energy to make the investment in your life?

Step 4

Creating an agreement concerning time and direction. Once a mentor has been found, it is a good idea to have a mutual agreement on the initial time and arrangement for meeting and working together. It could be a regularly scheduled breakfast or lunch once a week or twice a month, etc. It would be a good idea for the mentor to discuss with the protégé the goals and direction to be taken as this journey is begun. From this point, the mentor should have the freedom to direct the process along with input from the protégé.

The experience of being mentored is one which should be a part of the life of every person who desires to be in a leadership position in the church. I want to encourage every reader to pursue this relationship and experience the outstanding benefit which comes to men who are supported, encouraged and stretched though a quality mentoring relationship.

For Elders Who *Desire to* Mentor

What an exciting scenario at First Christian Church! The elders have each agreed to mentor one to four men this year who are potentially interested in becoming elders in the future! Think of the potential of the "deep bench" that would be developed if men were being mentored for future service. Consider the changed lives these men would experience as a result of the mentoring relationship. What a great move on the part of the present leaders!

Characteristics of Effective Mentors

First, the mentor has a healthy spiritual life. Mentors are not perfect people. But in their spiritual journeys, they usually are making progress and staying healthy, themselves. The adage is so true – "It is impossible for me to give away something that I don't possess." Staying on the growing edge is important for the person doing the mentoring. Being in the Word, praying and practicing other spiritual disciplines is absolutely critical in mentoring with effectiveness.

Second, the mentor has a clear vision. The mentor's vision for developing those coming up after him is vital. It comes down to developing disciples who develop disciples who develop disciples, etc. We are training younger leaders who will be stepping into the harness to lead the church as time moves forward.

Third, the mentor is committed through his time and attention. Mentors commit themselves. Mentors drive a stake. Mentoring calls for time, teaching, coaching, attention and communicating genuine concern to the protégé. There is a donation to be made and a price to be paid to see mentoring change someone's life. A good mentor takes the personal cost into account and moves forward.

Fourth, the mentor is committed to quality preparation. Good preparation is a key to many accomplishments in life. Sports, education and vocation all call for good preparation. Mentoring is the same. There is spiritual preparation to be made through prayer. There is content preparation to be made when the meetings for discussion and interaction takes place. The mentor is on time, prayed up, prepared and ready to connect. Good preparation is critical for effective mentoring.

Reflection Question: Rate yourself on a scale of 1-5 (1 being low, 5 being high) on the four commitments of a good mentor. Then, write a short paragraph describing your "readiness" to serve as a mentor.

A mentor is committed to . . .	Rating
a healthy spiritual life.	① ② ③ ④ ⑤
a clear vision.	① ② ③ ④ ⑤
through his time and attention.	① ② ③ ④ ⑤
quality preparation.	① ② ③ ④ ⑤

Two Key Aspects to the Mentoring Process

The two key aspects to the mentoring process are *formal mentoring* and *informal mentoring*. They are both important but different in nature. Jesus used both of these approaches when working with the disciples.

First, the Elder's Formal Approach To Mentoring – Jesus taught his disciples formally. Think of all the times when the disciples heard Jesus teach. The Sermon on the Mount in Matthew 5-7 is a good illustration. On many occasions, they heard Jesus teach in the synagogues, in people's homes, on the hillsides and by the seashores. Jesus taught in a structured, group oriented way, conveying content which the disciples needed to grow.

Our approach to this structured teaching opportunity also involves a planned meeting time for the mentor and his protégé(s). This is meeting normally happens every week at the same time (possibly even the same place, as well.) Mentoring meetings can take place at breakfast or lunch or another time that works for all parties involved. Since we have breakfast and lunch times in our normal schedule, why not use a meal time to connect? The meetings normally last an hour to an hour and a half (or whatever is agreeable to both parties.) Both mentor and protégé(s) make this meeting a *high priority* in their weekly schedule. Each scheduled meeting should involve several segments.

(1) *Re-entry* – The start of every meeting should involve a time of catching up with each other. This discussion can be informal and simply includes what has been going on in the previous week in each other's lives. I am in a group that begins with each man responding briefly to the question, "How are you doing today, really?"

(2) *Content Time* – Each meeting should involve a time in the Word or related topics. 1 Thessalonians 2:13 tells us, "For this reason we also constantly thank God that when you received the word

of God which you heard from us, you accepted it not as the word of men, but for what it really is, the word of God, *which also performs its work in you who believe."* The Holy Spirit works through the word of God to change lives, feed spirits and recreate Jesus Christ in men's hearts and minds. With tools such as *The Serendipity Bible, LessonMaker* and a good commentary on the Bible book you are studying, a leader can put together a good, discussion oriented study. Reading a good book on spiritual formation or leadership together (one or two chapters a week) can provide excellent fodder for discussion and personal application. Depending on where your protégé(s) are in their experience, why not share the leading of the study/discussion with each other or those in the group as the group progresses?

(3) *Prayer* – Every meeting should involve a time of prayer together. Mentor and protégé(s) should also pray for each other when apart during the week. Pray for each other's families, needs and prayer requests. Remember that intercessory prayer is taught and modeled in the Old and New Testaments, both. When meeting in a restaurant, why not look for a "back booth"? You can also simply pray together with your eyes open. Meeting together in a public place does not have to eliminate a quality prayer time, together. Prayer for each other is a key to the entire process of mentoring and discipleship.

Second, the Elder's Informal Approach to Mentoring – Jesus also used informal teaching times to train and develop his disciples. A few powerful experiences would include the exchange with the woman at the well, raising the widow's son at Nain, the interaction with Zaccheus in Jericho, the woman taken in adultery, the stilling of the storm, the changing of the water into wine at Cana, the raising of Lazarus from the dead in Bethany, the feeding of the five thousand, the washing of the disciple's feet and many more. In this approach to teaching, there is simply "life to life" exposure and connection.   No formal studies, tests or term papers were employed. Jesus does what he would normally do and the disciples watched. It is the power of informal teaching.

An elder who is mentoring one or more protégés has an outstanding opportunity to teach and influence informally. Here are a few suggestions:

&- *Hospitality* - Have the men with whom you are working into your home for a meal or desert. Why not have them bring their families, at times? Through time together, the men will see you interact with your wife and children. It is a great informal teaching opportunity.

&- *Sharing a common interest* - Sports provide an excellent occasion to share in informal teaching and influencing. Golf, tennis, racquetball, basketball or softball all offer great times of fellowship, camaraderie and sharing. Going to college or professional sports events also are enjoyable occasions for connecting.

A group of men from our church went to a wood working conference which was being held in our city on a Saturday. One of the men in the group shared with me that it was a very meaningful day for him. Spending quality time with men he admired, eating together and the hour's drive back and forth gave him time to interact and build a bridge to several men in the group. Other events could include white water rafting, a father and son trip involving fishing and camping out or a Friday evening, Saturday spiritual retreat.   Each of these could provide excellent opportunities for informal time together.

❧ Sharing a common task – Ministry projects can also provide open doors for informal influence. If you are teaching a Sunday School class or Adult Bible Fellowship, why not involve your protégé in the teaching event? Give him a portion of the lesson to present. Working a Saturday at the local church camp on their "work days" would be an open door to informal teaching. Being able to participate in something like a short term missions trip for a week or ten days would provide many occasions for powerful shared experiences.

The main idea behind informal teaching is simply that the protégé sees the mentor outside the formal teaching meeting. The mentor is sensitive to teachable moments and will take advantage of opportunities to instruct, influence, coach and encourage the men with whom he is working.

Reflection Question: Having read the chapter, prepare some reflections on how your eldership can provide mentoring as a means of leadership development within the congregation and the eldership itself. In a meeting, have each other share their ideas and create an actual plan for a mentoring ministry.

Conclusion

In conclusion, let us, as today's leaders in the body of Christ, commit ourselves to raising up our next generation of leaders. Let us give this area attention and focus in our work. The life and future of our church is depending on it. The church will always need men who love Jesus with all their heart, who live lives of extreme integrity, purity and honesty and who lead with great wisdom, discernment and boldness. It is one of the major keys to healthy churches who are fulfilling the request of Jesus our Lord as we move into all the world with His word.

📖 Resources

Excellent mentoring/discipling resources in addition to the references listed in the endnotes:

- Robert Coleman, *The Master Plan of Evangelism* (Revell, 1998)
- Bobb Biehl, *Mentoring: Confidence in Finding a Mentor and Becoming One* (Broadman and Holman, 1996)
- Kevin Greer, *Life To Life Discipleship* (College Press, 2000)
- Greg Ogden, *Transforming Discipleship* (IVP, 2003)
- Ron Bennett, *Intentional Disciplemaking* (NavPress, 2001)
- Bill Hull, *Choose the Life* (Baker, 2004)

Endnotes

[1]Lynn Anderson, *They Smell Like Sheep Vol. 2* (New York, Howard Books: 2007), 141.

[2]Greg Ogden, *Unfinished Business: Returning the Ministry to the People of God* (Grand Rapids: Zondervan, 2003)

[3]Howard Hendricks, *As Iron Sharpens Iron* (Chicago: Moody Press, 1995), 17-18.

[4] Margo Murray, *Beyond the Myths and Magic of Mentoring* (San Francisco: Jossey-Bass, 2001), 8.

[5] Lynn Anderson, They Smell Like Sheep Vol. 1 (New York: Howard Books, 1997), 39-40.

[6] Howard Hendricks, *As Iron Sharpens Iron* (Chicago: Moody Press, 1995), 16

[7] Ibid., 59-60

[8] Ibid., 60-71

Chapter 5

Taking Alongside: Leading by Shepherding

James Riley Estep, Jr.

"What exactly does an elder do?" Perhaps the most immediate response is "Shepherd the congregation!" Let's be honest, how many of our congregations have a portrait or a statue of Jesus depicted as a shepherd? Holding a lamb under one arm, walking with a shepherd's staff in one hand? We've all seen it. When one scans through the Old and New Testaments, the *shepherd* is perhaps the most common image of leadership and *shepherding* the most frequent mode of preparation for leadership encountered. To name a few the patriarchs were shepherds, Moses spent time shepherding, David was a shepherd (author of Psalm 23), the prophet Amos identified himself as "one of the shepherds of Tekoa", shepherds were present at Jesus' birth, and in an agricultural age as was the first century A.D. they were probably seen frequently and easily recognized. For whatever reason, shepherding flocks seem to prepare people for Kingdom service and leadership.

However, here is the contemporary problem: Most of us have not been shepherds nor have we ever been around sheep. The primary image of a leader in the Scriptures is an image with which we are virtually ignorant. In this absence, some have tried to put a new image in its place, something more familiar, like a CEO, manager, school teacher or principal . . . but God didn't choose images from the business or educational venues of their times, He chose the image of the shepherd to describe leadership in His Kingdom.

Many of our congregations do not appreciate or agree with the term "pastor" when applied to the preacher, but when elder's do not actively shepherd the congregation, we create a *defacto* pastor by our own omission of this ministry. As elders, you lead through shepherding God's flock. The ministry of shepherding is *not* optional in Scripture, but a fundamental expectation for those who would lead God's people.

Reflection Question: Have you ever had to take care of animals? Whether livestock or the family pet, what are some of the routine and extraordinary responsibilities they require of you? What if you were going out of town, what kind of instructions would have to be given the pet-sitter? Now, think of this as your shepherding of people . . . what all does (or should) it entail?

Biblical Lessons Learned from Shepherds

Fortunately, my brother-in-law is in fact a farmer who raises sheep, and is also an elder. Through him, I have had first-hand experience with a flock and see in him what it means to be a shepherd of the flock. As one studies the Scriptures, several principles of shepherding both sheep and people surface directly and indirectly from the text. *First*, elders reflect the person and ministry of Christ when they serve as shepherds. When Peter encourages elders to "be shepherds of God's flock" (1 Pet. 5:2), he employs the title "when the Chief Shepherd appears, you will receive the crown of glory that will never fade away" (1 Pet. 5:4). He reminds the elders that Jesus is in effect the head of their guild, the master shepherd from which they have learned their trade and to whom they are responsible for their service.[1] Jesus identified himself as "the good shepherd" and "the one shepherd" (John 10:14, 16) of God's flock, and as elders we now partner with him in shepherding. [2] Shepherding is not just a responsibility of the eldership, but rather a means of reflecting Christ-likeness in their leadership to the congregation.

Second, shepherds perform best when they have a vested interest in the flock. For example, flocks are tended by family (Gen.

4:4, 30, 40; 29:9; 31:6; 1 Sam. 16:19; 17:15; Ez. 34:12) are more highly regarded as being good shepherds; as opposed to flocks under the supervision of a hireling (1 Sam 17:20; Isa. 56:10-11; Ez. 34:8-10; Zech. 11:15-17; John 10:11). The practice of hiring individuals to tend one's flocks led to the image of shepherds becoming detestable, as reflected frequently in ancient Jewish literature. As elders, we must assume these responsibilities willingly as an appointment by God. Peter admonishes, "Be shepherds of God's flock that is under your care, serving as overseers — not because you must, but because you are willing, as God wants you to be . . ." (1 Peter 5:2a). As elders of the congregation, you are in an entrusted position to shepherd God's flock, one that cannot be readily relinquished to someone else.

Third, shepherds assume the responsibility for caring for the needs of the sheep, recognizing that they cannot always provide or care for themselves. As one reads Psalm 23, notice how much the Divine shepherd provides for His people. Sheep need to be led to food and water (Gen. 26:18-22; 25:32; 29:3; Num. 27:1-17), and have a tendency to wander away and not able to find their way back (Ez. 34:6-8; Luke 15:3-7). As shepherds of God's flock, elders are tasked with providing for the spiritual life of the congregation, even when their needs seem minor or trivial. This is why the Bible speaks of the unenviable prospect of being "sheep without a shepherd" (Num. 27:17; 1 Kings 22:17; 2 Chron. 18:16; Ezek. 24:5-8; Zech. 10:2; Matt. 9:36; Mark 6:34), meaning they are helpless and hopeless.

Fourth, protecting the flock was a shepherd's responsibility. Shepherds often used a rod or staff (numerous images of a shepherd's staff, including Ps. 23:4), as well as a sling (1 Sam. 17:40) as weapons to defend the flock. In fact, while Scripture often paints a very negative picture on dogs, in the context of shepherding they are given their only positive acclaim (Gen. 31:39; 1 Sam. 17:34-35; Isa. 31:4; Jer. 5:6, Amos 3:12). As one reviews the qualifications for elders, the explanation for the qualifications are often in the context of an elder's protective tasks by standing against heresy, divisiveness, or any threat to the congregation. Paul exhorted the Ephesian elders, "Keep watch over yourselves and all the flock of which the Holy Spirit has made you overseers. Be shepherds of the church of God, which he bought with his own blood. I know that after I leave, savage wolves will come in among you and will not spare the flock. Even from your own number men will arise and distort the truth in order to draw away disciples after them. So be on your guard! . . ." Acts 20:28-31a).

Fifth, a shepherd is recognized by his sheep. Jesus illustrated, "I tell you the truth, the man who does not enter the sheep pen by the gate, but climbs in by some other way, is a thief and a robber. The man who enters by the gate is the shepherd of his sheep. The watchman opens the gate for him, and the sheep listen to his voice. He calls his own sheep by name and leads them out. When he has brought out all his own, he goes on ahead of them, and his sheep follow him because they know his voice. But they will never follow a stranger; in fact, they will run away from him because they do not recognize a stranger's voice" (John 10:1-5). How recognizable to the congregation are you? The sheep know their shepherd because they have heard his voice, they have grown familiar to his presence, and recognize him as their shepherd. Would the congregation in which you serve recognize you as one of their leaders?

Reflection Question: How well do you embody these five biblical principles of shepherding? Using the chart below, not only rate yourself, but also provide some explanations or instances that illustrate the rating.

Principle	Rating	Explanation/Observation
Christ-likeness	① ② ③ ④ ⑤	
Vested interest	① ② ③ ④ ⑤	

Responsible for Care	① ② ③ ④ ⑤	
Protector/Guard	① ② ③ ④ ⑤	
Recognized by Flock	① ② ③ ④ ⑤	

Discuss how the eldership as a whole perhaps fulfills all these principles when serving together as shepherds of God's flock.

Shepherding as a Mode of Leadership

Why not cattle? Why did God choose sheep? I mean, why not be the herd of God rather than a flock? *Simple but significant distinction*: You *lead* sheep and *drive* cattle. You lead by being out in front, you drive from the rear. No one has ever heard of stampeding sheep; since they will simply part the way and let you run through them or just move aside while you pass by the flock. God used the imagery of shepherd-sheep-flock intentionally. How does one lead by shepherding?

Shepherd vs. Rancher? A classic church leadership distinction reflects the work of a shepherd. The shepherd approach to leadership assumes that every task is their own personal responsibility. On the opposite side of the spectrum is the rancher, a leader of shepherds, who assumes responsibility for the assigned tasks, but realizes that he need not be the one to actively engage it. The first is a more hands-on leadership role, while the other is more administrative and equipping in its approach to providing leadership. Both assume responsibility for the tasks of shepherding, but either work solo or in concert with others to fulfill our ministry.

An effective elder must be both a shepherd and a rancher. On occasion, based on his giftedness or opportunity, the elder must be the shepherd, directly involved in the ministry of the church. On other occasions, he must recognize his own limitations, but not relinquish his responsibilities as an elder; and must assume the role of the rancher, overseeing others in fulfilling the ministry task. They are in essence teaching others to be shepherds, raising the up into one day possibly serving as an elder. To employ a more contemporary image, an elder must be a player-coach . . . one that is actively engaged in the ministry of the congregation, while also guiding and equipping others to serve alongside him in fulfilling the role of leader. The   relation-ship of leadership-style and congregational health is *symbiotic*. Leadership-styles can promote or retard the congregations health, growth, and effectiveness. In a smaller congregation, elders can be shepherds; but as the congregation grows, elders mush morph toward the rancher model. Failure to do so will in effect impose restrictions and limitations on the congregation, because shepherds cannot single-handedly keep up with all the needs of the congregation. Likewise, as elders begin to intentionally move more toward a rancher-mode of shepherding, they equip others to do the ministry of the church, and hence the congregation becomes more effective and healthy, which promotes growth. As Figure 5.1 demonstrates, as a congregation morphs, the elder's shepherding style must likewise morph; and as elder's shepherding style morphs, the congregation's potential for growth likewise morphs.

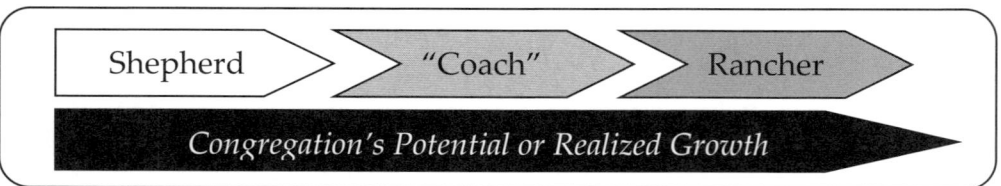

Figure 5.1: Shepherding and Church Health

In short, elders are in a position to aid the congregation's health, as well as impede it, based on their chosen shepherding stance.

But, how does the task of being a shepherd over the congregation translate into being a leader? Much as the biblical portrait displayed about a shepherd, an elder who responds to God's call to serve as a shepherd of His flock leads through active engagement in the ministry of the church, providing nurture for the flock, guarding it from those who would do harm, and being recognized as a leader by others. Shepherding is indeed *not* a positional form of leadership, but one that is earned by the respect and recognition of the congregation in which he serves. Shepherds are leaders because the congregation sees in them the heart of a servant, one who is devoted to the congregation's well-being.

Reflection Question: Is your philosophy of eldership more of a shepherd, rancher, or combination? Explain and illustrate your response.

Practical Guide to Shepherding

But how does one actually go about shepherding a congregation? Exactly *how* do I shepherd God's flock? Shepherding is both responsive and proactive. Shepherds respond to the needs of individuals and families within the congregation (and sometimes even the community), as well as be sensitive to the unexpressed need that requires a subtle approach, or even provide instruction and guidance to strengthen and guard the flock of God. In short, it takes a caring individual who is willing to invest his life and faith in the lives of others. A balanced approach to shepherding is comprised of five dimensions. While as individuals we may not be gifted or able to fulfill all five to their fullest, as an eldership (or working in concert with others in the congregation) these means of shepherding can be maximized in the congregation.

First, an elder is responsible for providing *spiritual care*. Already we have seen the elder as a defender of the faith and a nurturer of other's spiritual lives. One of the elder's ways of shepherding is to provide for the spiritual development of the congregation. How? Praying for the congregation's need and specific needs of individuals within the congregation. Leading others in developing their prayer life or perhaps in the practice of spiritual disciplines (as discussed *Reflect*). Elders directly assuming a leadership role in sponsoring special spiritual events such as congregational prayers, fasts, or devotionals would also fulfill this dimension of shepherding.

Second, *physical care* is likewise a concern for a shepherd. "Is any one of you sick? He should call the elders of the church to pray over him and anoint him with oil in the name of the Lord. And the prayer offered in faith will make the sick person well; the Lord will raise him up. If he has sinned, he will be forgiven" (James 5:14-15). Regardless of one's theological questions about this passage, the notion of elder's actively calling on the sick is Scriptural. [The elders of my home congregation in Lexington, Kentucky, actually at one time practiced the James 5 oil anointing if requested by someone.] Elders can pray for those they visit, perhaps bring materials from church (such as printed literature from the church), or even magazines or something of interest to the individual, such as a book. Also, remember that you are not only ministering to the individual who is ill, but his or her family. Asking them if you can do anything is also helpful and demonstrates a pastoral disposition.

Third, knowing the congregation requires an elder to build *relationships* within the congregation. If the sheep are to recognize the shepherd, even by just his voice; and if a good shepherd is one who realizes when even just one "sheep" is missing; the elder is obviously expected to have strong ties to those within the congregation. In one of my ministries a woman expressed an unfortunate but insightful sentiment regarding the eldership. "If an elder were to come up to my door, I'd wonder 'Uh oh, what's wrong?'" The elders were seen as distant and aloof to those in the congregation, and this lack of relationship impeded their ability to be shepherds. While the next volume, *Enjoy His People*, will focus on the essential relationships of an elder, it is enough here to say that elders must have interaction with members of the congregation so as to facilitate the shepherding role.

Fourth, an elder provides shepherding through his *presence and direction* within the congregation. Chapters in this book address how elders lead through decision making and strategic planning. This too is a dimension of the shepherding role of an elder. Remember, Psalm 23 uses the familiar image of a shepherd as one who is present with the flock and also directs them to where they must go. An elder's shepherding of his congregation not only requires them to be respondent to its needs, but proactively providing direction. When elders are actively involved in the presentation of the congregation's future plans or make announcements of decisions to the congregation, they are shepherding through having an active presence and direction.

Finally, *feeding* the flock is an essential aspect of shepherding God's people. As already highlighted in Chapter 1, an elder is to be a learner. But this is not just for personal benefit or for him to be a receptacle of information; rather to equip him to instruct others. Elders feed the flock by teaching the Word to them. If elders are to possess wisdom, it is to be shared with those whom they shepherd; providing Godly counsel, orthodox instruction, and insights into Christian living.

Reflection Question: How well do you embody these five means of shepherding? Using the chart below, not only rate yourself, but also provide some explanations or instances that illustrate the rating.

Shepherding Means	Rating	Explanation/Observation
Spiritual	① ② ③ ④ ⑤	
Physical	① ② ③ ④ ⑤	
Relational	① ② ③ ④ ⑤	
Presence/Direction	① ② ③ ④ ⑤	
Feeding-Instruction	① ② ③ ④ ⑤	

Discuss how the eldership as a whole perhaps fulfills all these means of shepherding to provide a more thorough ministry when serving together as shepherds of God's flock.

Models of Congregational Shepherding

If elders are to shepherd the congregation, how is it accomplished? Most congregations resort to a simple process of setting up a shepherding ministry. Like a mathematical equation, the numbers of congregation's members or families are divided by the number of elders, and hence each elder is given an equal portion of the congregation to "shepherd". While this may be the easiest, it is indeed the least effective. The simple assigning of elders arbitrarily to given members of the congregation is equivalent to a stranger who has no involvement in your life suddenly appearing on your doorstep. Often times this person functions simply as an attendance-watchdog, whose contact with individuals is limited to when they have missed worship 2-3 times and in need of "follow-up". This approach also underestimates the practical value and Scriptural mandate of shepherding. There must be a better way.

A better approach is based on *affinity* rather than "mathematically" or arbitrarily contrived divisions of responsibility. Affinity means that the elder and those to whom he directly shepherds have something in common. While one could quickly retort, "We all have Christ in common!" Yes, but having something else as well, such as a common interest, such as a social club, hobby, past-time, or even workplace provides a natural means of making contact. A congregation still needs to be concerned with the regular attendance of its members, ad especially of its newer members; but when done through pre-existing relationships based on common interests, shepherding is more nature and almost expected. A casual, "Hey, missed you at the Sunday School Christmas dinner. We're having a New Year's party at my place, interested?" from a co-worker at the water cooler is far more effective than, "Hey, where were you last Sunday?!?" by a virtual stranger from church.

In this instance, shepherding would be accomplished by accessing the complex network of relationships that exists in every church. Elders may be part of different small groups (broadly defined, such as any group that forms relationships between individuals in the congregation). If an elder is involved in any such groups, it would be rather easy for them to assume a shepherding role over his peer participants. It can also be accomplished by an elder's general involvement in the congregation's ministry. Their presence and knowledge of the congregation would prove invaluable as a means of tapping the relationship networks that pervade the church. As such, an elder may either directly shepherd an individual, or be a rancher, engaging the services of another who is in relationship with a member in need to provide more direct shepherding. Another way to provide comprehensive shepherding for the congregation is through "zone-pastoring". It is an endeavor to establish *neighborhoods* through the church. An elder may preside over a geographic area of the community in which the church members live; but rather than arbitrarily assigning individuals to elders as previously critiqued, the elder develops a pastoring team (rancher-mode) of individuals in his area to not only respond to needs of church members, but even sponsor events such as cookouts, Christmas parties, etc. that establish a congregation-based neighborhood. In any of these one fact is obvious: Shepherding is based on relationship. It requires the elder to be a man who does indeed care about people. An uncaring-shepherd is an oxymoron. An elder must both directly and indirectly provide for the comprehensive shepherding of the entire congregation through the natural relationships within it.

Reflection Question: How coordinated and comprehensive is your shepherding ministry? How is it organized? How well does it serve the needs of the congregation? What improvements might be made in the near future?

Conclusion

Spend some time with sheep! You'll gain an entirely new appreciation for the image of shepherding. Spend time with *your* sheep! Perhaps the simplest way to start shepherding is to mingle with members, to spend time before and after service just touching base with one another, spending time with those you lead as a shepherd. When I did, I gained entirely new appreciation for what Isaiah wrote of God, "He tends his flock like a shepherd: He gathers the lambs in his arms, and carries them close to his heart; he gently leads those that have young" (Isa. 40:11). As elders called to serve as shepherds of God's flock, may we too take this calling to heart and lead His flock.

Endnotes

[1] Cf. Adolf Deissman, *Light from the Ancient Near East*, trans. Lionel R. M. Strachan (Grand Rapids, Michigan: Baker Book House, 1965), 99-102.

[2] Jesus is also described as a shepherd in Hebrews 13:20, "May the God of peace, who through the blood of the eternal covenant brought back from the dead our Lord Jesus, that great Shepherd of the sheep."

Chapter 6

Taking to Task: Leading through Church Discipline

David Roadcup

"Therefore, I exhort the elders among you, as your fellow elder . . .
shepherd the flock of God among you. . . and when the Chief Shepherd
appears, you will receive the unfading crown of glory." (1 Peter 5:1-4)

The New Testament's teaching about the position of elder describes what an elder is expected to do as a primary leader in the church. An elder is to act as a shepherd to the flock. He is to manage the life of the church, to watch over the doctrine and guard the church from false teaching. He is to use his spiritual gift(s) to lead and strengthen the church. Elders are also responsible for the overall well-being of the church. They are to "keep the ship from hitting the rocks." They are to care for, oversee and nurture the "soul" of the congregation. This means that they are acutely aware of what is happening in the life of the church, knowing the successes and victories and also the problems, struggles and difficulties of the church's daily life and ministry. Part of that overall responsibility is to, with great care and serious prayer, oversee any church discipline situation which might present itself.

This chapter is included in this volume to assist elders and staff in the proper execution of biblical church discipline. Discerning church discipline, when done with prayer, clarity, fairness and communication, can result in the strengthening of a brother or sister who is struggling in his/her spiritual walk. It can also preserve the integrity, unity and health of the congregation, following the clear direction of Jesus, the Head of our church.

Exactly what do we mean when we use the term, "church discipline"? Marlin Jeschke defines church discipline as the following: "Church discipline refers to the ministry of discipling a Christian brother or sister whose spiritual health and life are endangered by a particular act or attitude."[1] Carl Laney states that "church discipline is the confrontive and corrective measures taken by an individual, church leader, or the congregation regarding a matter of sin in the life of a believer.[2]

The Biblical Injunction Concerning Church Discipline

It is clear that Scripture teaches us that discipline is to be part of the life of the church. Numerous examples and texts in the New Testament from Jesus and Paul both instruct leaders in the need for discipline and how it should be effectively accomplished. A classic text from Jesus' teaching is found in Matthew 18:15-17. Jesus tells us, "If your brother sins, go and show him his fault in private; if he listens to you, you have won your brother. But if he does not listen to you, take one or two more with you, so that by the mouth of two or three witnesses every fact may be confirmed. If he refuses to listen to them, tell it to the church; and if he refuses to listen even to the church, let him be to you as a Gentile and a tax collector." The clarity of this instruction cannot be missed. This plan that Jesus lays out is practical and effective. He gives us a clear process for working through difficult, relational problems and involves the church in the solution.

God undoubtedly indicates that discipline will be part of the life of the church through the example of Ananias and Sapphira in Acts 5:1-11. In a powerful and focused manner, the Lord teaches us that impure motives, lying and deception cannot be part of the lives of members of the body of Christ. (It is important to point out the significance of this event taking place in the New Testament as opposed to the Old Testament. Old Testament narratives explain to us that God would take extreme measures when necessary to get someone's attention. Here in the New Testament, He does the same, indicating His seriousness when it comes to the issue of following His commands.)

Paul directly deals with the discipline issue in 1 Corinthians 5:1-13. He writes to the Corinthian church and addresses the problem of the church member who was "living with his father's wife" (assumed to be the man's step-mother). Paul writes to Timothy and instructs him to "admonish the unruly, encourage the fainthearted, help the weak, be patient with everyone" (1 Thes. 5:14). To Titus he writes, "These things speak and exhort and reprove with all authority. Let no one disregard you" (Titus 2:15).

From these texts and many others, it is apparent that church discipline is to be part of God's plan for biblical and effective church management. As elders, the Lord is expecting us to oversee and lead the church in this area. In this particular day and time, church discipline is all but gone from most congregations. In many congregations, church discipline is not frequently required. But when situations requiring discipline present themselves, functioning elders follow Scriptural guidelines to help believers through properly executed discipline in love.

Occasions for Church Discipline

Listed below are a sampling of situations, when presented in the life of a church, that must be addressed by her leadership. This is not meant to be an exhaustive list but major areas of concern.

When a believer is participating in activities or lifestyle which is defined by Scripture as immoral and against the clear teachings of Scripture. When someone who confesses Christ as Savior is participating in willful, wanton, continual sin with no regard for repentance, Scripture is clear as to the responsibility of the church to seek that person out and work with them. 1 Cor. 5:11 states, ".......you must not associate with anyone who calls himself a brother but is sexually immoral or greedy, an idolater or a slanderer, a drunkard or swindler. With such men, do not even eat." (For further study, see Rom. 13:13-14; 1 Cor. 6:9-10; Gal. 5:19-21; Eph. 4:31; 5:5; Rev. 21:8; 22:14-15).

There are many and various examples of disobedient behaviors into which a believer might fall. Some of those could include:

- A person being arrested for embezzlement involving his or her work or business.
- A person committing fornication or adultery.
- A couple who decide to live together outside the bonds of marriage.
- A person or couple living in a homosexual relationship.
- Someone involved in spousal or child abuse.
- A believer who falls into drug, alcohol, sexual or some other form of addiction.
- A person who struggles with habitual lying.
- A person regularly participating in the viewing of or addiction to pornography.
- A contentious person who continually causes fighting or disruption among others.
- A person who continually participates in gossip, which results in personal hurt and injury to another.
- Someone who struggles with extreme criticism or negativity.

These and other examples are behaviors which need to be prayed for and given attention to when it comes to church discipline.

When a member of the church is teaching or promoting false doctrine. Acts 20:28-31 – "Be on guard for yourselves and for all the flock, among which the Holy Spirit has made you overseers, to shepherd the church of God which He purchased with His own blood. I know that after my departure savage wolves will come in among you, not sparing the flock; and from among your own selves men will arise, speaking perverse things, to draw away the disciples after them."

(Also see Rom. 16:17; Gal. 1:8-9; Eph. 5:6-7). The apostles Paul and John repeatedly admonish us as elders and staff to know what is being taught from our pulpits, in Sunday School classes and Adult Bible Fellowships, Small Groups, youth programs and other teaching events in our church.

Someone might say, "That could probably not happen in our congregation. We know our people." A ministry friend of mine told me that his church had started a very successful, church-wide, small groups ministry. The groups were being well attended and leaders were fulfilling their responsibilities. The ministry leader was  having lunch on a Sunday afternoon after services with a couple he had recently baptized into Christ. He inquired as to how they were enjoying their new small group. They responded positively. They did mention to him that they had concerns over the material the group leader had chosen for them to study together. It was a book he had read a number of years ago. They could not remember the name of the book but said it was published by a group called "Watch Tower." Upon checking, my friend discovered that a converted Jehovah's Witness was teaching the group and just thought that the book "had a lot of good material in it." It is important that we carefully watch what is being shared with our people in their groups and studies.

When a believer is causing significant disruptions of order within the church. Titus 3:10 – "Warn a divisive person once, and then warn him a second time. After that, have nothing to do with him." There are people who have named the name of Christ who, because of various reasons, cause division, strife and discontent among other church members. This cannot be allowed to go on if we want our church to be healthy. An on-going, constant negative attitude on the part of a church member is a good example of this behavior. Someone who hurts other people through gossip or back-biting is another. The point being made here is not referencing healthy disagreement and spirited discussion from a difference of opinions. This problem usually involves anger, bitterness, jealousy and a spirit to do harm and cause division within the congregation. Good elders will move on this issue carefully, firmly and without delay. Remember, one continuously negative, hurtful, cutting person, couple or family can do great harm to the life of a church in a very short time. No church is perfect. All churches can use improvement. There is a healthy, productive way to interact about differing ideas, new trends and approaches. But a divisive person who is intent on causing damage to the church must be confronted and dealt with.

Reflection Question: Reflecting on your experience as an elder, have there been occasions where such instances occurred in your congregation? How were they addressed (or why were they not)? What were the outcomes of addressing it (or not)? What did you learn from these instances?

Purposes of Church Discipline

There are five important spiritual and logical reasons why the Lord asks us to carry out discipline in the church.

To Honor Christ

The most significant way we can honor Christ is to accept Him as Lord and Savior. The second is to be quick to obey whatever he asks us to do. We bring honor to him when we obey. Obedience always honors Christ. Is church discipline distasteful? Is it difficult? Does it take time? Is it a draining experience? Is the experience full of angst, personal struggle and stress? The answer, of course is – Yes - by all means! It is all of the above. But we must keep in mind that Jesus has given us a command and directive. When a lamb strays and is in trouble, we, as shepherds, must respond. It means we pay the price of going through the process of prayer, contact, dialogue and attempted restoration. It means doing hand to hand combat with the enemy to save one of our own. Eternity may actually be in the balance for those with whom we will work the work of restoration. It is worth it. It is obeying Jesus by responding to his specific request.

To Reconcile and Restore the Fallen

In his book, *Biblical Church Discipline*, Daniel Wray states, "The goal in every type of discipline, whether it be gentle correction, admonition, rebuke, or excommunication, is always the restoration of the offender (Matt. 18:15; 1 Cor. 5:5; Gal. 6:1)."[3] To rescue a brother or sister from sinful practices and restore him or her to a fruitful walk in Christ should always be one of our main objectives in discipline

 situations. Discipline should never be simply for punishment or retribution but should always be to restore and heal. Jesus clearly indicates this in Matthew 18:15 and Paul reiterates the same in 1 Corinthians 5:5, 2 Corinthians 2:8 and Galatians 6:1. John Calvin wrote, "Although excommunication also punishes the man, it does so in such a way that, by forewarning him of his future condemnation, it may call him back to salvation."[4]

The story of the Prodigal Son in Luke 15 tells us of the joy of the father as he sees his son return from the "foreign land." In the same way, the church should "rejoice" when a fallen brother or sister repents and returns to the fellowship. When true repentance and recommitment are present in a believer's life, the church should model the forgiving heart of the Lord. That person should be restored to fellowship.

To Maintain the Integrity and Purity of the Church

As long as I live, I will never forget the scene. The televangelist's face covers the TV screen. He weeps as he pleads for forgiveness. He apologizes to God, his family, his church and his viewers for his moral failure. Forgiveness may have been granted, but the damage, which would take years to repair, has been done.

The world is always watching the church. It has from the beginning and will continue to do so. In our day of instant, world-wide media, it is not just the neighborhood or the city that is alerted to the church's failures; entire nations find out as fast as the blogosphere can carry the news.

The world is not easy on the church. It never has been. They are enemies and opposites. We all know the world will fire on the church whenever there is an opportunity. This is why the fall of numerous religious TV personalities has taken such a heavy toll on the church's credibility.

John Stott's comment on the church's struggle in this area is insightful. He states, "The secular world is almost wholly unimpressed by the Church today. There is widespread departure from Christian moral standards. So long as the Church tolerates sin in itself and does not judge itself.....and fails to manifest visibly the power of Jesus Christ to save from sin, it will never attract the world to Christ."[5]

We will continue to struggle in this area because the church is made up of humans who make mistakes. But this fact should not stop us from trying to maintain the highest level of personal and corporate purity and integrity possible. Every leader and every person in the church should be aware of how their personal influence and reputation affect the perception of the world toward the body of Christ.

A loving, wise, consistent approach to this biblical doctrine will greatly assist the church in her pursuit of purity and integrity before a watching world.

To Discourage Others from Sinful Practices

1 Timothy 5:20 tells us, "Those who continue in sin, rebuke in the presence of all, so that the rest also may be fearful of sinning." In certain instances, the elders must come before the congregation to share with them the necessity of removing someone from the body. Each disciplinary situation must be handled individually. Some are better handled privately. Some must be brought to the church as a whole. This must be done with great care and preparation. Through this process, members of our church will understand that the leadership is obedient to what the Lord has asked them to do. As believers witness the practice of discipline in the church, it will serve as a motivation to help them to avoid sin themselves.

To Not Grieve God

In Revelation 2:14-25, Jesus tells the church in Pergamum that he has something against them. They were entertaining false teachers and allowing immoral practices in their congregation. He tells them to repent or he will "come to them quickly." From this case of a lack of direction by the elders at Pergamum, we see the Lord's response. It is possible to lose the blessing and anointing of the Lord on your congregation. Whether it is "sin in the camp" (Josh. 7) or allowing sin to continue in the church, the Lord can and will remove His Spirit and blessing from a church. Obedience always invites the Spirit of the Lord to be present.

Common Mistakes with Church Discipline

There are mistakes that elders or staff members can make when attempting to do productive church discipline. Church leaders should be aware of each of the following:

Misunderstanding or incorrect application of Scripture. Elders and staff need to invest time, study and thought into a study of church discipline. This could be done on a retreat or through a series of identified meeting times. Then a policy statement, based on Scriptural teachings, needs to be put on paper. The statement should then be incorporated into the church's by-laws and staff handbook for practical and legal purposes.

A failure to get all the facts and vital information. One of the most important parts of the church discipline process is the obtaining of reliable information about the person, their situation and the accurate verification of those facts. The false accusation of a member of the church would be disastrous. Careful interviews and research into the situation is an absolute necessity and should be done with great care and humility.

Difficulty with confrontation or lack of confrontation skills. Those who do the visit(s) with the one offending should be able to face a confrontation and execute it well. Very few people enjoy confrontation. It can be distasteful and stressful. But effective confrontation, when done with prayer, humility and love can produce very positive results and ultimately result in the restoration of a believer. In another section of this chapter, we will discuss the process of effective confrontation.

Lack of consistency (Perceived favoritism) – It is crucial that when Scripture has been examined and church discipline policy has been written that it be applied to all members of the congregation without partiality or favoritism. To practice church discipline when necessary with some and not others would be a prescription for disaster.

Mishandling of the process resulting in rumors, hearsay and loss of confidentiality. When a situation presents itself and is not handled in a timely fashion and with due diligence, problems can arise. Delay or neglect can result in rumor, hearsay and gossip. Because people are people, a possible loss of confidentiality can occur. After a situation has presented itself, it is best to move judiciously through the process and bring it to completion.

Lack of action through fear of reprisal. In the litigious culture in which we live, there can always the threat of lawsuit or reprisal of some kind. This issue will be addressed later in this chapter. Seeking legal advice may be wise, depending on the people involved and the situation presenting itself. We do need to consider moving forward in discipline situations with great care while making sure we are fulfilling the Lord's will in keeping the church pure.

 ⌖ **Reflection Question:** Which of these five has hindered you personally or as an eldership from engaging in positive church discipline? What has been the result of yielding to such "barriers" and making such "mistakes"?

Two Types of Church Discipline

There are two approaches to church discipline that should be identified and considered. The first is called *Preventive* discipline. Preventive discipline is doing everything we can *before* the offense or pattern occurs to teach, motivate and encourage believers in their spiritual growth. There are several suggestions which deserve our attention:

First, there should be a strong emphasis in the life of the church on the Word of God. Members should be exposed to the Word on a regular basis. Powerful sermons and teachings that have been carefully prayed over and prepared should be presented. Members of the body should be taught how to start and maintain a daily time of being in the Word to assist them in feeding themselves between weekend services.

Second, an effective shepherding ministry should be developed in the life of the congregation. Once a person comes into the church through accepting Christ or transferring membership, there should be an effective and identifiable plan in place to assimilate them into the life and ministry of the church. A big part of an effective plan involves a church wide Small Groups ministry. Small and mid-size (Sunday School or Adult Bible Fellowships) groups are one of the most effective approaches in helping people develop spiritually. This would include involvement in ministry teams, music ministry, sports, youth groups, men's, women's and single's groups. Each of these and others are all important in the shepherding effort.

Third, involving people in service is also a positive way to connect people, stimulate their growth and help them to find a deeper relationship to Christ. Identifying and using their spiritual gifts and talents will bless the church and strengthen the believer.

Fourth, while disciplining members after the infraction has occurred is important, strategizing and planning beforehand concerning what we can do to grow, motivate and protect our members from failing into sin is a healthy way to shepherd our people.

The other approach to church discipline is *Corrective* discipline.[6] Corrective discipline takes place after the offense has occurred. There are two scriptures which should be examined when studying corrective discipline. The first is Matthew 18:15-17 and second is 1 Corinthians 5:1-13.

Church Discipline and Matthew 18:15-17

In Matthew 18:15-17, with amazing brevity, Jesus gives us a clear concise method concerning how to perform an act of discipline. It reads, "And if your brother sins go and reprove him in private; if he listens to you, you have won your brother. But if he does not listen to you, take one or two more with you, so that by the mouth of two or three witnesses every fact may be confirmed. And if he refuses to listen to them, tell it to the church; and if he refuses to listen even to the church, let him be to you as a Gentile and a tax-gatherer." Step by step, Jesus gives us the formula.

The offense occurs - "If your brother"

When there is an offense, Jesus says that the one offended approaches the offender and initiates a discussion. The use of the word "brother" indicates that there should be a positive and loving attitude on the part of the initiator. It indicates "family" and "support" which should be found in the culture of every church. Paul, in 2 Thessalonians 3:15 points out that we are to see the Christian taken in sin "not as an enemy, but admonish him as a brother." Warmth, genuine concern and love should characterize out attitude and emotional frame of reference when approaching a situation involving discipline.

The *attitude* we have as we approach an erring fellow Christian is very crucial. If our attitude says, "We are going to teach you a lesson" and carries with it an air of superiority, the outcome may not be the one desired. Paul also tells us in Galatians 6:1 that we are to approach an erring brother "in gentleness." This means with a spirit of self control, humility and love. He also tells us that we are to be careful, lest we, upon hearing of the details of the situation (especially in the areas of sexual sin, greed, etc.) also fall into temptation ourselves.

Identifying the problem - "sins"

Something in the brother's life has "missed the mark." He has broken spiritual laws the Lord has requested we keep. Whether he is in a state of denial or simply resolved to be involved in sin, our sincere, Godly concern motivates us.

The heart-felt confrontation - "Go to him"

Jesus urges us to approach the brother and confront him with his sin predicament. Don Baker, in his excellent book entitled, *Beyond Forgiveness*, has this to say about the step of confrontation: "It is right here that most corrective relationships break down. Confrontation, to many, is extremely difficult. To 'speak the truth in love' to an offending brother requires more than an insensitive accusation. More than a perfunctory rebuke. More than an unsubstantiated assumption. Confrontation, or the act of addressing the problem of sin in the brother's life, must be prayed over, thoroughly thought through and the approach carefully planned. It must not be done impulsively or in anger since it is the first crucial and cautious step toward the restoration of a Christian brother or sister. Since the instinctive human response to any suggestion of sin is denial, the first step in confrontation is critical."[7]

 Confrontation is difficult! Expect it to be the most stressful part of the process. Elders know that effective leadership always requires effective confrontation which hopefully will lead to redemption. Confrontation is always difficult, but it is the step that brings us to the place where real healing and restoration can begin to happen. According to Jesus, it is essential to the process.

Careful preparation should always precede confrontation. Let me suggest a plan to follow before you encounter the person face to face.

1. Immerse the entire situation in fervent prayer. Ask the Lord to prepare your hearts well as the heart of the person with whom you will be meeting. Effective preparation has prayer at its foundation.

2. Purge your motives. Be sure you have considered the situation carefully in your heart and mind. Rid yourself of any anger or feelings of hostility before you approach the person with whom you are going to talk. Make certain your central reason for meeting

with him or her is your desire to see the person restored in their personal walk with Christ.

3. Before you approach the brother, think carefully through what you will say. If need be, write it out. Be prepared. Remember that your tone of voice and facial expression are critical in your interaction. You will communicate more through your tone of voice and facial expression than through your words.

4. Make contact with the person. You can call and make an appointment or simply visit unannounced. Which method you choose depends on the person and the situation. Usually, however, it is best to contact the person and make an appointment for the visit.

5. After breaking the ice, come to the point. Explain exactly what the problem is. At this point, be sure to express your sincere concern, ask the brother for his response and listen carefully to what he or she says.

Fourthly, this passage indicated the need for reproof.

The confrontation in love - "reprove him"

To expose and convince one of sin is the meaning of the word "reprove" here in Matthew 18. Reproof is the gentle, loving word of warning that tells the offender that someone knows and cares about the sin in his life. It suggests that someone is willing to take the risks involved in confrontation and to spend the time necessary to help.

One on one - "in private"

There is no need to embarrass the brother if he is willing to repent. Confidentially can be very important to restoration and healing. This process is not to be done in public or before a group of co-workers. It is to be done one on one. The desired response - "If he listens to you, you have won your brother" This is the goal of the entire process. Repentance - forgiveness - healing- restoration - the brother is reclaimed.

The alternative response - "but if he does not listen"

If there is no repentance, you are to make a second visit following the same approach with two or three others. If the brother continues to deny, rationalize, make excuses or display anger at your coming, then the matter is to be taken to the church body and explained. If the person still does not repent, the person is to be viewed as "a Gentile and a tax-gatherer." They are to be removed from the church until they repent.

Church Discipline and 1 Corinthians 5:1-13

The city of Corinth during the time of Paul was one of the most sinful and debauched cities of the whole of Asia Minor. Worship of idols and sin of all kinds abounded. But even with sin being rampant, what was happening in the Corinth church was even shocking to the Corinthians. A believer in the church was "sleeping with his father's wife". This was, no doubt, his step mother but the practice was taboo, even to the Corinthians. The practice also broke Jewish law and Roman customs.

In 1 Corinthians 5, Paul deals with the church and this scandalous problem. This passage is unique in that Paul instructs the church to excommunicate one of her members. In this specific situation, the church has become "arrogant" and has not "mourned" over the man's sin. The church has not moved to remove the man. Paul gives very clear instructions to the church and criticizes the church for her lack of concern over the issue. They are to "remove the wicked man from their midst" (verse 13).

The positive outcome is that 2 Corinthians 2:6-8 tells us that the church followed Paul's instructions and the man caught in sin repents and it restored to fellowship. What important lessons can we learn from this passage?

First, the church *must* practice discipline when necessary. Paul strongly chastises the church for allowing rampant sin to exist in their midst.

Second, when sin is severe, it requires movement on the part of the church. A mild rebuke would not serve in this situation. The sin needed to be dealt with swiftly and with serious measures. 1 Corinthians 11: 21-30 tells us that when we avoid giving attention to damaging sin in the church, we can cause weakness, sickness and spiritual death.

Third, when the sin is public information, it requires public attention. When information has spread throughout the church and the community about grievous sin in the life of a member, the sin should be dealt with in a public manner. The situation should be brought before the church by the leaders. This is done for two important reasons: (1) to encourage the person caught in sin to sincerely repent and to be restored and, (2) To warn the church that sin cannot be tolerated in the church.

Legal Issues in Church Discipline

Whenever church discipline is exercised, there is always the issue of legal action against the church to be considered. The space in this volume does not allow a detailed discussion of this issue, as critical as it is to this topic.

Listed below are numerous resources (books and websites, etc) which the reader will find helpful in carefully handling legal issues:

- www.brotherhoodmutual.com has an entire section dedicated to risk management resources. At this website, you will find articles, checklists and many other helpful resources in the SafetyCentral section of the website.

- www.ChurchSafety.com. has many valuable resources.
- The links below will also take you to valuable information:
  - LegalAssistance Q&A #9 - "How can we guard against liability related to church discipline?"
  - SafetyCentral Article - "Responding to Lawsuits Arising from Church Discipline"
  - The Law of Church and State in America - Chapter 3 - Church Membership (by Dean M. Kelley)
  - *Church Discipline and the Courts* by Lynn R. Buzzard and Thomas S. Brandon, Jr. (Tyndale, 1987), which is good in principle but may need legal updating.

If a legal problem is in the making, searching for a qualified attorney who has experience in the area of church law will be a key in advising and consulting.

Part of the care, shepherding and development of any church is a careful approach in executing church discipline. It is an important tool when needed and useful in building a healthy church. Following scriptural guidelines and bathing each situation in prayer will guide us in handling each person with wisdom and discernment to fulfill the end goal of discipline, which is the restoration of the believer to an even more fruitful and joyful life in Christ.

📖 Suggested Resources

- Jay E. Adams, *Handbook of Church Discipline* (Zondervan Publishing, 1986)
- John White and Ken Blue, *Healing the Wounded* (InterVarsity, 1985)
- Marlin Jeschke, *Discipling in the Church*, (Herald Press, 1988)
- Donald Wray, *Biblical Church Discipline* (Hazell Watson and Viney Ltd, 1988)
- Don Baker, *Beyond Forgiveness* (Multnomah Press, 1984)
- Ken Sande, T*he Peacemaker (Updated Version): A Biblical Guide to Resolving Personal Conflict*: 2003, Baker Books

- Norman Geisler, *Christian Ethics: Contemporary Issues and Options*: 2010, Baker Academic; 2 edition
- Wayne C. Raychard, *Biblical Discipline in a Cross-cultural Setting: Who is Empowered to Act in the Absence of an Established Local Church?*: 2009.
- VDM Verlag Dr. Müller Ezekiel B. Kephart, *A Manual of Church Discipline*: 2009, BiblioBazaar
- B. Y. Stuart PhD LCPC, Principles *of Spiritual Leadership: Assuming Your Responsibilities (Volume 96)*: 2009, CreateSpace
- Bill Zimmer, "How to Practice Church Discipline": 2003, www.biblebb.com/files/MAC/SC03-1040.htm
- Marlin Jeschke," How Discipline Died": 2005, www.christianity today.com/ct/2005/august/13.31.html
- Interview by Mark Galli, "Shaping Holy Disciples" (Mark Dever says church discipline is not about punishment or self-help): 2005, www.christianitytoday.com/ct/2005/august/ 14.32.html
- John Ortberg, "Spheres of Accountability" (The dynamics of discipline in the megachurch): 2005, www.christianity today.com/ct/2005/august/16.33.html
- Ken Sande, "Keeping the Lawyers at Bay" (How to correct members while staying out of court): 2005, www.christianitytoday.com/ct/2005/august/17.34.html
- Interview by Stan Guthrie, "The Evangelical Scandal" (Ron Sider says the movement is riddled with hypocrisy, and that it's time for serious change): 2005, www.christianitytoday.com/ct/2005/april/ 32.70.html
- Interview with Ken Sande, "Taking Church Membership Seriously" (Why it's time to raise the bar): 2005, www.christianitytoday.com/le/currenttrendscolumns/leaders hipweekly/cln50418.html
- Interview with Ken Sande, "Church Discipline Really Works (pt. 1)" (When you make it loving and redemptive): 2005,

www.christianitytoday.com/le/currenttrendscolumns/leadershipw
eekly/cln50124.html
- Interview with Ken Sande, "Church Discipline Really Works (pt. 2)" (How to find courage - and avoid lawsuits- when confronting sinning believers):2005,
www.christianitytoday.com/le/currenttrendscolumns/leadershipw
eekly/cln50131.html
- Website: www.Peacemaker.net (Equipping and assisting Christian and their churches to respond to conflict biblically)

Endnotes

[1] Marlin Jeschke, *Discipling in the Church* (Scottsdale, PA: Herald Press, 1988), 17.
[2] Carl Laney, *A Guide To Church Discipline*, (Grand Rapids: Bethany House Publishers, 1989), 14.
[3] Daniel Wray, *Biblical Church Discipline* (Great Britain: Hazell Watson and Viney Limited, 1988), 3-4.
[4] John Calvin, *Institutes of the Christian Religion*, Book 4, Chapter 12, Section 10 (http://www.reformed.org/master/index.html?mainframe=/books/insti tutes/entire.html).
[5] John Stott, *Confess Your Sins: The Way of Reconciliation* (Waco, Texas: Word, 1974), 49.
[6] For an excellent in-depth discussion on Corrective discipline, see Jay E. Adams' *Handbook of Church Discipline* (Grand Rapids, Zondervan, 1986), Chapter 3.
[7] Don Baker, *Beyond Forgiveness* (Portland, Multnomah, 1984), 37.